EISENHOWER, GOLF, AND AUGUSTA

DAVID SOWELL

For a Very Special Trio:

Sullivan, Carrigan, & Grant

INTRODUCTION

The route to golf's Hall of Fame has taken its members down many different paths. But none has been more unique than that of 2009 inductee Dwight D. Eisenhower. His journey was by way of the Oval Office and it did not begin in earnest until he was in his late fifties.

As one would expect of a unique journey, Ike's trek to the Hall had its origin in unique circumstances. It began in late 1944, during the Battle of the Bulge, with his initial encounter with an Augusta National member in the clubhouse of a bomb-ravaged French country club. It idled for the next four years, until he made his first trip to the Augusta National Golf Club. When Ike first set foot on the grounds of the Club as a guest, he was 57 years old and at best a casual golfer. He departed 10 days later as a member and on a rapid path to becoming a full-fledged golfoholic.

During this first Augusta visit in 1948, Ike was hosted by a group of five. This group, which would subsequently add two more Augusta National members, would become known as "the gang." They were an assorted mix of high achievers. Three had found fame and fortune from very humble beginnings; one started out as a meter reader, one as a traveling clothing salesman, and the third as a B-list vaudeville performer. Another of the seven was a college dropout who had been born with a golden spoon in his mouth that was said to have been immediately jerked out by his father and melted down for its bullion. Two in the group had high-powered college degrees.

The final member of this group was an Atlanta native who had two college degrees, one in mechanical engineering from George Tech and another in English literature from Harvard. Passing the Georgia Bar exam after attending Emory University Law School for just three semesters, he was also licensed to practice law. In 1930, he was one of four finalists for *Time Magazine's* Man of the Year award. The other three finalists were Joseph Stalin, Adolph Hitler, and Mohandas Gandhi. The winner was Gandhi.

This man's name was Bobby Jones, the greatest golfer ever to play the game and one of the most popular figures ever in American sports. What had placed him in contention for *Time's* prestigious award in 1930 was his achieving a feat no one thought possible: winning all four of golf's major championships – the British Amateur, the British Open, the United States Open, and the United States Amateur – in the same year.

Soon after completing this extraordinary achievement, dubbed the Grand Slam, Jones retired from competitive golf at the age of 28. Shortly thereafter, he set out to build the ideal golf course. He ultimately picked Augusta, Georgia as its location. Once the Augusta National Golf Club opened in 1933, the aura of Bobby Jones, the beautiful and engrossing course he created, and the Masters Tournament, seemingly overnight made Augusta National the course most golfers in this country would like to play while the Masters became the tournament that the game's top players would most like to win.

Passing over a long list of Army brass whose rank and qualifications outdistanced Ike's, General George Marshall, Chief of Staff of the Army, had made Ike the equivalent of a Captain's Pick in the Ryder Cup when he chose him to be America's commander against Hitler. Even before V-E Day, Ike was being touted as presidential timber. When the war ended, this sentiment steadily increased. Nowhere was the feeling that Ike belonged in the Oval Office any stronger than among his new gang of friends and their fellow members of Augusta National Golf Club.

In late 1950, President Truman asked Ike to return to Europe to head up the North Atlantic Treaty Organization (NATO), headquartered in Paris. Ike accepted. He served there for almost 14 months. While there he golfed frequently on the courses around Paris, and with him for a third of these rounds were members of the gang and other Augusta National members who had journeyed over to stoke the coals for Ike to make a run for the presidency as a Republican in 1952. Their efforts, along with the efforts of others, paid off as Ike threw his hat into the ring. With his Augusta National gang running point, he won the Republican nomination in a hard-fought battle and then crushed his Democratic opponent, Adlai Stevenson in the general election.

Setting the tone for what the next eight years would be like, Ike flew to Augusta the day after he was elected for a 10-day vacation at Augusta National. Six months after his inauguration, triggered by two more trips to Augusta National and his spending Wednesday and Saturday afternoons when in Washington teeing it up at the Burning Tree Golf club just outside the city, Ike set off a golf explosion in the United States. Surveying the expanse of empty courts at his tennis facility at Forest Hills in New York City, the operator described the impact the new president's golf had had on his business. He said in a voice tinged with remorse, "It's Ike who's done it. I remember just as late as last year you couldn't get on these courts without a reservation a couple of days in advance. With President Eisenhower playing golf, it changed the whole sports picture. Have you checked the public golf courses around here? You wait a couple of hours to get on the first tee. That's an honest fact. You can't get near a golf course on weekends."

An old Republican Party adage for Ike's two terms in the Oval Office has been, "Ike led this country, dominated the planet, contained the Soviet Union, solved all sorts of problems, and played golf." While the first four points of this axiom would be open to debate, the last point would not.

From his slipping out to Burning Tree Golf Club for a quick nine after delivering a State of the Union Address, handling a Mid-East crisis from his office above the pro shop at Augusta National, or as he played a round, keeping track by walkie-talkie of the progress of evacuating his vice president, Richard Nixon, from a hostile situation in Venezuela, Ike always seemed to find the time to tee it up. The appointment files labeled

"Golf" in the Dwight D. Eisenhower Presidential Library in Abilene, Kansas, show he played almost 900 rounds during his eight years in office. This total would have easily surpassed 1000 if he had not been sidelined by a heart attack, intestinal surgery, elbow problems, bursitis, and a stroke.

Visitors to the Library can see a section of the flooring from the Oval Office that was taken up after he left office. It is pock-marked from his golf spikes, where he walked into the office after his late afternoon practice sessions. He had these sessions almost daily on the South Lawn of the White House. Working with his favorite club, the eight-iron, he would hit shots in the direction of the White House fountain and the ornamental pool.

Ike, Golf, & Augusta chronicles Ike's obsession for the game of golf, his love of Augusta National, and his relationships with his golf gang. It details how golf was intertwined with both of his presidential election victories, and the big events of his eight years in office, from the Army-McCarthy Hearings to the U-2 crisis. It also covers the effect his golf had on his family, his staff, his allies, and his opponents, both domestic and foreign.

1

TEEING IT UP

Today, a team of Secret Service agents would have this responsibility. But on election night in 1952, the assignment fell to a sixty-year-old investment banker. If central casting was looking for the perfect fit for the role of a small-town undertaker, he would be their guy: slightly above average height, hawk-nosed, bespeckled, large ears, his weight just barely out of the undernourished category, and dark thinning hair combed straight back. His appearance and reserved demeanor gave no hint of his power and influence. He was Clifford Roberts, the commander of a very elite group: the membership of the Augusta National Golf Club.

Roberts was standing guard at the door of a room at New York City's Waldorf-Astoria Hotel. On the other side of the door, stretched out on a bed catching a few z's, was an Augusta National member who had just won the presidency of the United States in a landslide—General Dwight D. Eisenhower. While they were waiting for Ike's opponent, Adlai Stevenson, to concede, Roberts had ushered the next president of the United States into one of the unoccupied rooms on the Eisenhower campaign's floor, so he could get some rest before giving his victory speech.

With Roberts at the point, a small but very powerful group of Augusta National members had provided the key push, both to get Ike into the presidential race and in his campaigns, first for the Republican nomination and then in the general election.

Ike's first encounter with an Augusta National member had, appropriately enough, taken place at a country club, albeit a heavily bombed one. It occurred during World War II, during the Battle of the Bulge. Augusta member Bill Robinson was the vice president of one of the then leading newspapers in the United States, the *New York Herald Tribune*. Before France fell to the Germans, the *Tribune* had published an English-language edition in Paris for 10 years.

Soon after the Allies liberated Paris, Robinson arrived there to set the wheels in motion for the *Tribune* to resume publishing its Paris edition. He ran up against some regulations that Ike had imposed concerning the do's and don'ts of doing business in Allied-occupied territory. Robinson requested a meeting with Ike to seek relief from a few of these regulations. The arrangements were worked out for the meeting to take place at Eisenhower's headquarters, which was in the clubhouse of what was left of a war-torn country club near the town of Rheims, northeast of Paris. But a few days before the meeting was to take place, the Battle of the Bulge began. Robinson expected his appointment to be cancelled. When he inquired about it, he was told it was still on.

When the meeting began, Robinson apologized to Ike for taking up his time while a big battle was taking place. Ike told him not to worry about it. He was confident that his forces would take care of the situation, and he was now developing plans for actions weeks after the current battle. The two men hit it off during the meeting and they became good friends.

In the spring of 1948, shortly after Ike had retired from the military, Robinson invited Ike down to Augusta National for a golf vacation. There to greet them upon their arrival were the club's co-founders, Bobby Jones and Cliff Roberts, and two founding members, Robert W. "Bob" Woodruff, the chairman of the Coca-Cola Company and W. Alton "Pete" Jones, president of the oil and gas giant Cities Service Company (now CITGO).

Soon after the United States had entered World War II, Bobby Jones had enlisted in the Army and served as an intelligence officer. He had met Ike in the spring of 1944 in England, during the preparations for the D-Day invasion. Bob Woodruff had already entertained Ike for a weekend soon after the war ended at his plantation at Callaway Gardens near Atlanta. Ike had done a lot for the Coca-Cola brand during the war. He had pushed for and received portable Coke plants for his troops in Europe, much to the consternation of the other soft-drink makers. He also gave Coca-Cola one of the biggest free endorsements it ever received. On his initial visit back to the States after Germany's surrender, Ike received an enormous welcome home. His every move was double-covered by the press. At one of his first public appearances, he was asked if there was anything he wanted. He replied, "Could somebody get me a Coke?" One was quickly provided and after he finished it, he said he had another request: "Another Coke."

Pete Jones, along with Roberts, was meeting Ike for the first time. He had been one of the country's heroes on the home front during World War II, spearheading the construction of an oil pipeline from Texas to the East Coast that was completed in time to support the D-Day invasion. He was also heavily involved with the building of a secret explosive production facility in Arkansas and the construction of an aviation fuel refinery in Louisiana.

Ike's visit to Augusta lasted for ten days. After spending his days on the course he and his new friends would gather after dark for what would become the norm for whenever they got together—a full night of bridge. During his early years in the Army, Ike's prowess at the poker table became well known. He reportedly borrowed the funds to buy his wife Mamie's wedding ring and then retired the debt through his poker winnings. Legend has it that Ike was concerned that his reputation as a card shark was hurting his career. So he gave up poker and replaced it with bridge. His skills at bridge soon rivaled his poker-playing ability and it became his favorite indoor activity.

Although he had arrived at Augusta National as a guest, Ike departed as a dues-paying member and with Cliff Roberts now handling his personal finances. Soon after leaving Augusta, Ike surprised almost everyone when he chose as his first civilian job the presidency of Columbia University. His new job worked out well for his friends from Augusta National as Cliff Roberts,

Bill Robinson, and Pete Jones were all based in New York City, as well as another New York City-based Augusta member who would join the gang, Ellis Slater. They got together regularly just outside the city on Wednesday afternoons and Saturdays for golf at Blind Brook Country Club.

Ellis Slater was the president of Frankfort Distilleries, the makers of Four Roses blended whisky. Once Ike entered the political arena, Slater, being in the spirits business, always kept a low profile when he was with Ike and was particularly careful not to be photographed with him.

Ike had barely gotten his foot in the door at Columbia when President Truman asked him to become a part-time troubleshooter at the Pentagon, in hopes of ending squabbling among the commanders of the individual branches, mainly over the amount of appropriation each would receive. By February 1949 the situation had not improved, so Ike, at Truman's request, took a short-term leave of absence from Columbia to work full-time at the Pentagon as the temporary chairman of the Joint Chiefs of Staff.

Several weeks later, Ike became ill in his Washington hotel room with what was diagnosed by his personal physician as a severe case of acute gastroenteritis. On President Truman's suggestion, Ike was flown, on Truman's plane, to Key West, Florida, to recuperate. Mr. Truman was Key West's biggest fan. His first visit there had been made reluctantly in November 1946 at the insistence of his physician, so he could shake a lingering cold. When he arrived, he immediately fell in love with the locale. Over the remaining six years of his presidency, Truman vacationed there as often as he could. While there, he swam, fished, and enjoyed plenty of late-night poker. He also enjoyed long walks on the streets of Key West. In the process, he created a fashion craze in casual wear, with his fondness for wearing very colorful Hawaiian-type shirts on these strolls.

A couple of weeks later, and a few days after Sam Snead won the 1949 Masters, Ike's doctor placed a call to Cliff Roberts at Augusta National. Ike had shown little improvement at Key West, so his doctor asked Roberts if he could bring Ike up to Augusta National. Roberts' answer was an emphatic "yes."

Ike arrived the following day. Roberts described Ike's arrival in his book, *The Augusta National Story*:

When I first saw Ike, I was shocked. He was weak to the point of almost trembling. What had happened in the short time since I last saw him in New York was alarming. But just to get a look at the club seemed to lift his spirits. The first day he could do no more than walk a few holes, the next day he was on the practice tee for an hour, and the third day he played nine holes of golf. His ability to recuperate was astonishing.

Ike stayed at Augusta for almost a month. When he departed, he appeared to be as good as new.

As mentioned in the introduction, since before V-E Day there had been ongoing talk about Ike as a possible presidential candidate. Being career military, Ike's political leanings were not clearly discernible. Both major political parties were interested in him as a candidate. But as time went by after he left the Army, it became clear that Ike's thinking about the direction he believed the country should be taking placed him in line with the Republican Party. There was plenty of excitement about the possibility of him being the party's candidate for president, especially among the members of Augusta National, a GOP stronghold.

In late 1950, President Truman asked Ike to take over command of the North Atlantic Treaty Organization (NATO), headquartered just outside Paris. Ike agreed to take the position and took another leave of absence from Columbia.

Early in January of 1951, Ike made a quick trip over to Europe to meet with the leaders of the member nations in NATO. He returned to the States to brief President Truman and Congress on those meetings before officially taking command at the NATO Headquarters later that month. After those briefings, Ike flew to Puerto Rico to have a golf outing with Cliff Roberts and several other Augusta National members before heading back to Paris for his new assignment.

Once at NATO Headquarters, it didn't take long before Ike was a regular on the Paris-area golf courses. He did have to make an adjustment in one aspect of his golfing. He had always been prone to let the "expletives fly" after a bad shot. Since the caddies in France were almost all female, he made an extreme effort, though not always successful, to keep from having those type of outbursts.

According to logs in the Pre-Presidential files at the Eisenhower Library, Ike played 72 rounds of golf during the approximately 14 months he was in charge of NATO. As mentioned in the Introduction, for a third of those rounds in Paris, a member of Augusta National Golf Club was in the group, stoking the coals in hopes of firing up Ike for a presidential run. Cliff

Roberts and Bill Robinson made several lengthy visits, while five other Augusta members had shorter stays. Also, Roberts didn't want Ike to feel left out during Masters Week at Augusta National in 1951, so he placed some money down for him in the club's gambling pool and kept him apprised on how his wager was doing by telegram each day.

As the 1952 campaign season began to unfold, Ike seemed to be straddling the fence as to whether to enter the race or not. What seemed to tip the scales was when he was shown a film clip of an "Eisenhower for President" rally in Madison Square Garden that drew 15,000 enthusiastic supporters. Shortly after seeing the film, Ike threw his hat into the ring.

It appeared at first that Ike may have waited too long to make his decision. Senator Robert Taft of Ohio, the son of former president William Howard Taft, had started his campaigning long before Ike entered the race and appeared to have the inside track for the nomination. But by the time the primary season was over and the two candidates' forces headed to the party's convention the first week of July in Chicago, it was a virtual dead heat.

When he would recall covering the 1952 Republican Convention, a gleam would return to the eyes of broadcast news legend Walter Cronkite. It was the kind of old-time, no-holds-barred convention that the current news media would give their eye teeth to cover. This epic struggle for the GOP nomination had it all: political rancor, arm-twisting, fisticuffs, backslapping, deals and rumors of deals, and quiet diplomacy.

All of Ike's supporters from Augusta National were committed to the fight. The most dauntless member of the

Augusta National legion was Bobby Jones. Several months after Ike's first Augusta visit in 1948, Jones had been diagnosed with a spinal disease that would get progressively worse. Now, four years later, the effects of the disease had reached the point where he needed a cane to assist him in walking. But Jones was right up on the front lines in the thick of the battle, calling on delegates who were still up for grabs. His efforts, along with those of the rest of Ike's forces, ultimately won the day. They came up nine votes short of the nomination on the first ballot. Then it was announced that the Minnesota delegation planned to change its 19 votes to Ike on the second ballot. Since this would give Ike the nomination, other delegations, not wishing to be on the losing side, switched to Ike as well, giving him a huge margin of victory. The next day, Richard Nixon was selected for the number two spot on the ticket.

Two weeks later, the Democratic Party held their convention in Chicago and selected Adlai Stevenson as their nominee and John Sparkman, a United States senator from Alabama, to be his running mate.

Ike held a strong lead in the early polls. The GOP ranks, however, were more than a little anxious about the impact of Ike's golf on his campaign. And who could blame them, given the experiences of the last two golfing Republican presidents: Taft and Harding.

Theodore Roosevelt had hand-picked William Howard Taft to succeed him as president. Roosevelt believed that Taft had all the tools necessary to keep the country on the right path. But Roosevelt did recommend that he clean up one aspect of his personal life before the 1908 election campaign: He wanted him to dump golf.

The 51-year-old Taft had been a state judge, the Solicitor General of the United States, a judge on the United States Court of Appeals for the Sixth Circuit, the Governor-General of the Philippines, and President Roosevelt's Secretary of War. But he had never run for an elective office. On an early campaign swing through the Midwest, Taft created quite a stir when he took a few breaks to play golf. Mail began pouring in to TR at the White House, critical of the preoccupation with the game by his hand-picked candidate.

TR fired off a letter to Taft with a dire warning about his golf. He wrote:

I have received literally hundreds of letters from the West protesting about it. I myself play tennis, but that game is a little more familiar; besides, you never saw a photograph of me playing tennis; photographs on horseback, yes; tennis no. And golf is fatal.

Taft chose to ignore TR's advice and even turned up the focus on his golf. To a large gathering at a campaign stop in Wosley, South Dakota, he said this:

They said that I have been playing golf this summer, and that it is a rich man's game, and that it indicated I was out of sympathy with the plain people. I want to state my case before the bar of public opinion on the subject of that game of golf. . . .It is a game for people who are not active enough for baseball or tennis, and yet when a man weighs 295 pounds (he was understating his weight by about 50 pounds) you have to give him some opportunity to make his legs and muscles move, and golf offers that opportunity.

Taft went on to handily defeat his Democratic opponent, William Jennings Bryan.

To clear the deck for Taft in the public's eye, TR decided to leave the country for a year to safari in Africa. This action had the reverse effect. The papers covered TR's exploits in Africa as if he were still the president of the United States. And of course the press coverage was easy to understand because TR's activities were of more interest to the public than the activities of the current president as it seemed all Taft was doing, while TR was trekking around Africa killing lions, was trekking around golf courses in Washington and at vacation resorts. And the Taft stories were almost always the same. He played golf with a business tycoon, or his golf score for a round was such and such, or he sprained an ankle playing golf. As a result his golf game became an anathema to the press and to the public as well.

By his own admission, Taft was not suited for the presidency and he used golf as an escape. To make matters worse, he did not like dealing with the press. He afforded them very little access to him, which compounded his image problem. One of the favorite lines bantered around about Taft was, "he hardly gets fairly settled down to golf before presidential duties interrupt him."

By early 1912, Theodore Roosevelt had become so disenchanted with Taft, he decided to challenge him for the Republican Party nomination for that year's presidential election. Taft managed to defeat Roosevelt's challenge at the Party's convention but Roosevelt regrouped and mounted a campaign as a third-party candidate.

It was a very tough campaign featuring the two former allies and the Democratic nominee Woodrow Wilson. In the closing weeks of the race, it became apparent that Taft would finish in third place. On the eve of the election, Taft returned to his hometown of Cincinnati, Ohio, to cast his vote. On Election Day, he played a round of golf and then went to the polling booth to vote. Wilson won easily, taking 435 electoral votes to Roosevelt's 88 and Taft's eight.

Twelve years later, during the Republican Party Convention in Chicago, a deal was cut in a smoke-filled hotel room in the wee hours of the morning that gave the party's 1920 nomination for president to Warren G. Harding, a United States senator from Ohio.

Mere weeks after the convention, Harding's campaign was in a tailspin and an urgent call for assistance was placed to Chicago. Harding wasn't calling the party bosses; he was far beyond their help. He needed the Chicago Cubs!

Harding had ingested a huge dose of political poison; he had allowed himself to be filmed playing golf by a crew from a newsreel service. In 1920, golf was gaining steam in its popularity, particularly in certain pockets of the country, but its image with the overall population was very negative, as it was still generally viewed as a game for the privileged.

As soon as the newsreel footage began to roll in movie houses around the country, the Harding campaign was inundated with negative reaction. One United States senator who was backing Harding fueled the campaign's mounting dismay. He stated that he had been in a packed theater where the newsreel, which showed Harding teeing off and putting in fancy knickers, was shown. He reported that there was not one applauding set of hands in the entire place.

Harding's team feverishly put together a plan to stage an event that they believed would be the perfect antidote for the golf film. They were going to put Harding back in front of the cameras enjoying a game that was as mainstream American as you could get—baseball. The owner of the Chicago Cubs was a Harding backer and arrangements were made with him to bring the Cubs to the candidate's hometown of Marion, Ohio, for a game against a team of locals.

The campaign ran stories a few days before the game about Harding's love for baseball. The pieces chronicled Harding's playing days as a bare-handed first baseman, and detailed how he was once a major stockholder in a professional team in the Ohio State League.

A crowd of 7000 packed the small Marion ballpark and greeted Harding with a rousing welcome when he arrived. With the cameras rolling, he went straight onto the field and warmed up the Cubs' pitcher, future Hall of Famer Grover Cleveland Alexander. After the warm-up session, Harding made a few brief remarks to the crowd, threw out the game's ceremonial first ball, and then whooped it up in the grandstand like the contest was the seventh game of the World Series. The Cubs won the game 3-1 but Harding was the real winner. When this newsreel footage hit theaters, it more than cancelled out his golfing gaffe.

Harding golfed in secret for the rest of the campaign and defeated his Democratic Party opponent James Cox by a huge margin. Shortly after the victory, Harding took off for a lengthy golf vacation in Florida.

Cliff Roberts took the point in handling Ike's golf during the general election campaign.

Outside of his own hometown of Abilene, Kansas, nowhere was Ike's popularity any greater than in Denver, Colorado. His wife, Mamie, was a member of one of the city's most prominent families, and the Mile High City had welcomed with great enthusiasm Ike's placing his campaign headquarters there for his quest for the Republican nomination. Next to Augusta, the Cherry Hills Golf Club in Denver, the host of a number of golf's major championships over the years, was Ike's favorite. It was there he had played his first round of golf in 1925, while he was temporarily assigned to the Denver area as an Army recruiting officer.

Shortly after Ike had secured the Republican nomination, he received an invitation to play in a golf tournament at Cherry Hills called the Hillydilly. Although its name sounded rinky-dink, that was far from the case. Held in the late summer, it was the equivalent of the Masters for a select group of rich and powerful golfers from across the country and the stakes and the wagering were high. When Roberts got wind of the invitation, he advised Ike to decline it. He further advised Ike if he did play any golf not to wager any money but to play for golf balls instead. He was concerned that an alert photographer might get a picture of Ike paying off or collecting a wager after a round.

Roberts also advised Ike that he did not believe his membership in Augusta National would have any ramifications during the campaign, since he had been a member for four years before he entered the political arena. Also, it was Robert's thinking that although Augusta was an exclusive club, the popularity of Bobby Jones and the Masters Tournament offset that angle.

By no means was Roberts' advice limited to golf. He gave Ike his views on religion, scheduling, and fundraising. In terms of religion, Ike had been brought up a devout member of the Brethren in Christ Church, a denomination whose teachings focused on personal responsibility, the importance of disciple-ship and obedience, and the separation of church and state. In most cases, they often did not have a formal church building and met for worship in the homes of their members. In adult-hood, Ike had considered himself a non-sectarian Christian. Roberts was getting rumblings from Ike's backers over the fact that their nominee had no formal religious affiliation and they wanted him to join a church. Roberts made Ike aware of theses concerns but suggested they be ignored, as he was of the opinion that not having a religious affiliation was more of an asset than a liability in the campaign. Two weeks after his inau-guration, Ike became a Presbyterian. His baptism took place in a private ceremony in the nation's capital at the Washington National Presbyterian Church.

In terms of scheduling, Roberts did not want Ike to stretch himself too thin with speeches and public appearances. With television now in the mix with radio, Roberts believed it was more important how well Ike performed in his speeches, not how many he gave.

Regarding fundraising, Roberts voiced his concerns to Ike about the fact that too many of his campaign donations during the primary had come from big contributors in the northeast and he wanted to see a push for smaller donations from a larger, more geographically diversified group.

Ironically, it was through Roberts and fellow Augusta National member Alton "Pete" Jones efforts that funds poured into the Ike campaign in the Northeast for the primaries and for the general election. So much so that when the campaign ended, unused funds were returned to contributors. The success and resultant power of both these two men belied their humble beginnings.

Pete Jones was born in Webb City, Missouri. One of the first jobs he had as a youth was working in the local bookstore. The proprietor became upset one day over Jones' timidity when he assisted a prominent resident of the community with a purchase and gave him this advice: "Never let any man overawe you."

After high school, Jones enrolled in Vanderbilt University, but he had to drop out after one year because his mother became ill. He took a job as a meter reader for the local gas company and began studying bookkeeping through a correspondence school. He soon was working in the office as a clerk. After a short while, Jones was promoted to the position of auditor.

Nine years later, Jones' hard work and a series of acquisitions and mergers eventually landed him an executive position in New York City with the Cities Service Company, one of the country's leading companies in the natural gas and petroleum industry. Six years later, in 1927, at the age of 36, he took over day-to-day operations of the company. Two years after that, the company's stock price hit a high of $68 a share, but shortly after achieving that mark, the company was rocked to its core by the stock market crash of 1929. The stock price eventually plummeted to just 75 cents a share. Jones successfully guided the company through the Depression. It emerged from those financially turbulent times as one of the most solid companies in the nation, and Jones became one of the country's highest-paid executives.

Not only was Jones a founding member at Augusta National, he also purchased memberships for four of his friends, which was typical of his generosity. He never let anyone else pick up a restaurant check. When improvements were needed at Augusta National, he would offer to underwrite the whole project.

For a very wealthy man, Jones had some peculiar idiosyncrasies. When he traveled, he often carried in excess of $50,000 in cash with him. He refused to buy golf tees and would send his caddie foraging for some while he negotiated for strokes on the first tee. He also liked to see how many shaves he could get out of a razor. When he went on a trip, he would carry a large metal block to sharpen his razor.

Cliff Roberts's journey to wealth and power also began in a small town in America's heartland. He was born in Morning Sun, Iowa. His mother was a distant cousin of Frances Scott

Key, the writer of the lyrics to *The Star-Spangled Banner*. His father was a real estate salesman who always wanted to see what was on the other side of the next hill, so consequently the family moved frequently and eventually ended up in Texas.

Cliff never finished high school and took to the road selling men's clothing when he was about 16, and he did quite well at it. After several years, he decided New York City was where he needed to make his fortune. After one failed assault on the Big Apple, Roberts regrouped and tried again, but World War I got in the way. He went into the Army and ironically received his first exposure to Augusta, Georgia, as a result when he was sent to Fort Hancock, located just outside the city, for training. After completing his training, he was shipped over to the war's front in France and served as an ambulance driver.

Following the war, Roberts was able to get a foothold within the New York financial scene, despite his lack of formal education. He endured many ups and downs, including taking a beating in the crash of 1929. He persevered, however, and eventually forged a very successful place for himself on Wall Street, becoming a partner with the prestigious brokerage firm of Reynolds and Company.

In an extensive interview with the Columbia University Oral History Project after Ike's death in 1969, Cliff detailed how he had handled a situation during the 1952 presidential campaign that had the potential to be very damaging to the Eisenhower campaign.

On the late afternoon of June 5, 1944, Ike was driven down to the staging area of the 101st Airborne Division. In a few hours these paratroopers would be taking off to start the D-Day invasion with a night drop well behind the Germans' coastline defenses. The planners of the attack were projecting their casualty rate might be as high as 70 percent. When Ike stepped out of his car, he ordered the four-star license plate on his vehicle be covered and allowed only one staff officer to accompany him. Despite his attempted low-key approach, he was immediately recognized, and the airborne troops quickly began yelling and cheering. Ike told the troops they could break ranks and forget about military formalities. He worked his way over the huge area. As he made his way from group to group, a new round of cheers would erupt. The troops told Ike not to worry about them, their confidence was high.

Ike stayed at the field until the last plane was airborne. He then turned to his driver with tears in his eyes and said, "Well, it's on." Then he looked up at the sky filled with planes and added, "No one can stop it now."

Ike's driver was Kay Summersby, a shapely divorced former fashion model in her mid-thirties. She was a member of the British Army's Mechanised Transport Corps and had been assigned as Ike's driver shortly after he arrived in England to lead the Allied effort. She had been with him in North Africa, Egypt, and Sicily and she would be with him through the war's end. Throughout the time Kay was on Ike's staff, there were persistent rumors the two were romantically involved.

After the war ended, Kay moved to New York City. In 1947, she wrote a book about her experiences with Ike entitled *Eisenhower Was My Boss*. The book was certainly not a tell-all, nor did it produce the type of financial success Summersby had envisioned. Since the book produced no new fuel about a

Kay/Ike affair, talk about their war-time relationship moved to the back burner of the rumor stove.

Five years later and just as Ike's presidential campaign had begun, Kay popped up on the radar screen. According to Roberts, Kay had been in contact with close acquaintances of Ike about her personal situation. She was now down and out, working as a sales clerk at a department store in New York City. She also let it be known she was considering responding to recent overtures she had received about doing some more writing about her and Ike.

In the midst of Ike's run for the presidency was certainly not the time for more speculation about his war-time relationship with Kay to be on the front burner again. Roberts took care of the problem by sending Kay cash. The money was provided under the premise it was to be used to underwrite her expenses while she tried her hand at writing a play. Kay's desire to be a playwright quickly waned. Roberts then arranged for her to obtain employment at the New York City office of another Augusta National member. She soon became romantically linked to a successful stockbroker and dropped off the campaign's radar screen.

As the general election campaign unfolded, Ike consistently held a five- to seven-point lead in the polls. Six weeks before Election Day, Cliff was so confident of victory that he wrote the membership of Augusta National and advised them their access to the club would be restricted the two weeks immediately following the election. Because Ike was going to take a working vacation there as soon as the race was over.

Ike's victory was bigger than anyone had expected. On election night Stevenson was dragging his feet when it came to conceding defeat. This really irritated Ike. He did not want to take the stage for his victory speech until Stevenson had conceded. Ike's legendary temper was about to get the best of him. It was at this point Cliff decided Ike needed a time out. He ushered him into one of the campaign's unoccupied rooms to cool down and grab a few moments of rest. While Ike got in a quick snooze, Roberts assumed sentry duties just outside the door. About an hour later, word came that Stevenson had conceded and Cliff went in and woke up the President-Elect of the United States and escorted him down to Waldorf's ballroom to give his victory speech. When the final vote was tallied, Ike had won 55 percent to 44 percent and in the Electoral College the count was Eisenhower 442 and Stevenson 89.

The election returns that night had also been very good for three other Republican golfers. Swept into office with Ike was a single-digit handicapper named Barry Goldwater. He won election to the United States Senate from Arizona, upsetting veteran Democrat and Senate majority leader Ernest McFarland. In Connecticut, Prescott Bush, a two-time president of the United States Golf Association and the father of future president George Herbert Walker Bush and the grandfather of another president, George W. Bush, also won election to the United States Senate.

Last, but by no means least, in this trio was Jack Westland, the reigning United States Amateur Champion. He won in the state of Washington's House of Representatives Second District race, a seat that had been held by the Democrats for two decades.

In Chicago in 1931, at the age of 26, Westland had lost in the finals of the U.S. Amateur to Francis Ouimet, whose stunning upset of British golf legends Harry Vardon and Ted Ray 18 years earlier in a playoff in the 1913 United States Open had ignited the fuse for a golf explosion in America. The 1952 U.S. Amateur Championship took place in Seattle, Washington in late August. With the event being held practically in his backyard, Westland, now 47, decided to take a week off from his campaign in the Republican Primary to take another shot at winning the title. No one was any more surprised about his performance than Westland. He fought his way into the finals and then defeated a player who was 25 years his junior to claim the crown. In doing so, he became the oldest player ever to win the event.

Winning the Amateur gave Westland's primary campaign a big boost and he won the race in a convincing fashion. In the General Election Ike came to Westland's district and campaigned for him. To show his appreciation, Westland gave Ike the putter he used to win the Amateur.

2

AUGUSTA NATIONAL'S PULL

Twelve hours after Ike was awakened by Cliff Roberts to make his victory speech, a plane charted by Roberts carrying Ike and his entourage lifted off from LaGuardia headed for Augusta, Georgia. Ike would not be the first president-elect to take a golf holiday in Augusta. Forty-four years earlier and long before there was an Augusta National Golf Club, William Howard Taft had spent nearly a month there, playing golf at the Augusta Country Club and at a course in nearby Aiken, South Carolina, after he won election in 1908.

During the flight, Roberts sat down with Ike and solicited a promise from the President-Elect. Seeking to insure Augusta National would be the one place Ike could go for uninterrupted relaxation, Roberts requested that whenever Ike visited the club while in office, he would not leave the grounds, except to go to church. Roberts was anticipating a barrage of invitations of various kinds and he believed if Ike accepted one it would

open up the floodgates and create problems for him and
Augusta National. Ike agreed with Roberts and gave him
his word.

Most of Augusta turned out and lined the streets to cheer
Ike as his motorcade made its way from the airport to Augusta
National. Ninety miles away in Atlanta, Bobby Jones was at
home, wishing he could be at the club to welcome Ike. But his
doctors would not let him travel. Jones had campaigned tire-
lessly for Ike until three weeks before the election, when he was
felled by a heart attack on the sidewalk in front of his Atlanta
law office.

Once Ike and his party were inside the grounds at Augusta
National, Cliff assembled the press corps and advised them of
their parameters for covering Ike's stays at the club. A few of
these were:

- No list of club members would be made available.
- Pictures could be taken only on special occasions.
- No information on Ike's scores would be provided.

Cliff then directed the press corps to choose three from their
ranks to play the course, and these three were to share their
impressions of the course with the rest of the group.

During his stay, Ike spent his mornings working on matters
pertaining to the transition of power from Truman's administration to his and spent his afternoons playing golf. Most of his

work time was devoted to filling cabinet posts and other high-level positions. This was accomplished through coordination by phone with key advisors back at his transition headquarters in New York City. Ike did not like talking on the phone, so initially Cliff was handling the calls to and from New York. This setup proved to be too time consuming and was cutting into Ike's golf time. So after two days, Ike decided he would put aside his aversion to the telephone and handle the calls himself.

While at Augusta, Ike did make one job offer in person. His presidential campaign's motto of "I Like Ike" is one of the most popular of all times. Women were particularly drawn to Ike. In the presidential election, more women than men voted for him. One woman who jumped on the "I Like Ike" bandwagon early had been a lifelong liberal Democrat and she had been very active in the feminism movement. Her name was Ann Whitman.

Ann, 44, was five-feet-seven inches tall, slim, and attractive. She liked a good laugh and a good drink, preferably a martini, and she was athletic. In high school, she played on the school's championship basketball team. She liked horseback riding, was a huge baseball fan, and she had played some golf. She had been a secretary in New York City for 20 years. Unhappy with the course of the Democratic Party, she had become involved in the Citizens for Eisenhower organization early in 1952 and soon thereafter had signed on to work in the secretarial pool of Ike's campaign office in New York City. A few weeks before the Republican Convention in Chicago, she and a few other staffers took off for Denver to reinforce the staff at Ike's national headquarters. Just days after Ann arrived, Ike's regular secretary became ill. Being the only other person on staff who could take shorthand, Ann stepped in as a pinch hitter. Ike liked her from the start. When his regular secretary returned to the office, she was given another assignment.

While Ike was working half days at Augusta, Ann was putting in a full day and then some working on the transition in a small room near the men's locker room. Augusta National was far from the perfect place to be the hub of a presidential transition. Just finding a phone to use was a major accomplishment. It was while searching for an available phone that Ann had an up close and personal encounter with a club member, boxing great Gene Tunney. She made a wrong turn and stepped into the member's locker room where she bumped into Tunney, who was toweling off after exiting the shower. Her quest to find a phone ended at that point and she did an about-face and retreated to her little room.

It was in that small room late one afternoon that Ike finally got around to asking her to be his personal secretary at the White House. Everyone had assumed he would ask her, but it was the kind of formality Ike sometimes just assumed everyone understood was a given. Although she had misgivings about the effect it would have on her marriage–her husband working in New York City and she in Washington–she readily accepted the job. Ann later told a friend she had no real choice because during the campaign she had developed a passion for the excitement of life at the top. Ann, who in just a few months had gone from total obscurity to being a top assistant to the world's most powerful leader, would remain Ike's secretary for both of his terms in office and his first year in retirement.

Also joining Ike's team was a local Augusta black man that Cliff Roberts hand-picked. He went by the nickname of "Dead Man," a moniker he picked up as a young man when he was prematurely taken to the morgue after coming up on the losing end of a knife fight. His name was Willie Perteet. By night, Willie made the rounds of the Augusta bar and club scene, playing the drums in a band, and by day he was a long-time member of Augusta National's caddie corps. He was given the appointment of "First Caddie" and would be at Ike's side whenever he was on the Augusta National course.

When Willie told Ike the story of how he acquired his nickname of Dead Man, Ike told him dead men belonged in the cemetery and called him "Cemetery" from that point forward.

Due to his limited play during the long campaign, Ike's golf game was a little rusty when he arrived at Augusta. Ed Dudley, the pro at Augusta National who was considered one of the game's best instructors, worked with him on the practice tee for several days to help him get his game back in shape. He also joined Ike and Cliff for several of their earlier rounds during Ike's first week at the club. For each round of the second week of Ike's stay, golfing legend Byron Nelson, whose five major championships included two wins at the Masters, joined him on the course.

When Ike departed Augusta, wife Mamie was delighted with the rejuvenation the stay had given him. The campaign had been exhausting and she was particularly concerned about the bulging veins in his hands, forehead, and the back of his neck, which had disappeared during this stay.

Ike took the Oath of Office on January 20, 1953. His first

trip to Augusta National Golf Club as President occurred just over a month after his inauguration. He wrote a letter to Cliff Roberts on February 10, 1953. In the letter, he stated he had hoped to get down to Augusta for a long weekend on February 13th but had decided against it. His thinking was it would be bad public relations to take such a trip after being on the job for just three weeks, so he would wait until the second week in April to come down. Only a very limited number of golfers in the country who are capable of satisfying a desire to play Augusta National would know how powerful an urge it must have been. The urge was far too powerful for Ike, a man who had four years earlier kicked a three-pack-a-day cigarette habit, cold turkey. On February 26th, Ike's plane streaked down the runway at Andrews Air Force Base outside Washington and took to the sky. Its destination: Augusta, Georgia.

Close behind Ike's plane was a plane carrying the White House press corps. It made a slight diversion before landing, flying over Augusta National so photographers could take some aerial shots of the course. Ike's numerous trips to Augusta soon grew thin on this group. The city's heyday as a winter resort had long since past. Spoiled by Harry Truman's long winter stays in Key West, Ike's White House press corps had the same disdain for Augusta more recent White House press corps developed for Jimmy Carter's stays in Plains, Georgia, and George W. Bush's lengthy visits to his ranch in Crawford, Texas. The press was not alone in its discomfort in Augusta as many of Ike's staffers and some of the Secret Service agents shared these feelings. The most adamant of whom was Ann Whitman. She once declared Augusta, "was a place about which I have nothing favorable to say."

Those whose employment required them to join Ike in Augusta's chief complaint was their accommodations at the Bon-Air Hotel. It had once been the Waldorf-Astoria of the Augusta scene. Its past included one of the biggest snubs of a president in history. When he was in his late 50s, oil magnate John D. Rockefeller took up golf and soon became one of the nation's most enthusiastic players. In accumulating his vast fortune, Rockefeller's ruthless business practices had resulted in his being looked upon with extreme disfavor by a large portion of the country's population. When President-Elect Taft had arrived in Augusta for his post-election vacation, Rockefeller was also there and requested a golf game with him. Taft initially agreed. When Mrs. Taft heard about it, she hit the ceiling, fearing it would create a mountain of negative reaction and Taft cancelled the game. Mr. Rockefeller was not very happy.

A few years later, President Taft decided on the spur of the moment to take a trip down to Augusta for some golf. When he arrived at the Bon-Air, there were not enough rooms available to accommodate his entire party. Mr. Rockefeller was again staying at the Bon-Air and as was his custom, he had taken a whole floor of rooms, many of which were not occupied. A member of Taft's staff called on Mr. Rockefeller and asked if he would possibly give up a few of his unoccupied rooms for the President of the Untied States' party. He declined, forcing a sizeable number of Taft's entourage to find accommodations elsewhere.

By now, in early 1953, the Bon-Air's best days were well

behind it. Whitman and the others had plenty of complaints: hot water often came from both faucets; once the heat had been turned on, it could not be shut off; and room service was hopelessly lax. They found the most successful way to get breakfast was to stand in the hall and wait for a waiter to come by with a tray targeted for another room, then slip him a few bucks and take off with the tray. The big winner in that case might have been the person the tray had been intended for, as Ann described the food as being vile.

On this first trip as president, there was another reason Ike wanted to get down to Augusta National besides golf. He had something he wanted to personally present to Bobby Jones: a painting. Soon after Ike had taken over as president of Columbia University, Thomas E. Stephens, a noted artist, was commissioned to do a portrait of Mamie for display in the president's residence. While Stephens was working on Mamie's portrait, Ike became an interested observer. So much so, that soon after Stephens finished Mamie's portrait, he sent Ike a complete painter's kit. Ike was reluctant to take the plunge at first, but the more he dabbled in painting the more he liked it and it became his third-favorite pastime behind golf and bridge.

In late 1952, the United States Golf Association requested a portrait of Bobby Jones for the library of Golf House, its headquarters in New York City. Cliff Roberts raised the funds for the painting from Augusta National members. At Ike's urging, Thomas Stephens was commissioned to do the painting. The portrait, which was of a young Bobby Jones (circa his 1930 Grand Slam year) in his follow-through position, was unveiled at a special ceremony at Golf House with Jones present a few days after Ike was inaugurated as president.

Copying from Stephens' work, Ike had done his own version of the Jones portrait. He had begun working on it a few weeks before he took office and completed it at the White House, working on it during the evening in his study.

Ike presented the painting to Jones in a little ceremony on the lawn in front of the Augusta National clubhouse. Jones was visibly moved by Ike's gesture. A corner of the portrait bore the inscription, "'Bob' by his friend, D. D. E. 1953." Ike, on the other hand, acted bashfully about the painting, apologizing for a number of what he perceived to be imperfections. But many present, including a number of the press corps, thought the work to be rather good; especially from someone who had only been involved with painting for just a short time.

Ike was the first "Jock President" in the nation's history. At Abilene High School, he played football and baseball. He played football at West Point. And for the first ten years of his military career, a good deal of his time was spent coaching the football teams at the bases he was assigned.

In high school, the football team went undefeated his junior year, winning all seven games and allowing only one touchdown to be scored against them. At that time, high school athletics in Kansas was primarily left in the hands of the students. His senior year, Ike was elected to a very important position at Abilene High–president of the Athletic Association. It was in this post the man who would later direct the D-Day invasion obtained his first managerial experience, scheduling games, negotiating for equipment from local businesses, and arranging away-game travel–which could sometimes mean slipping covertly onto a freight train.

But Ike's transition from high school athletics to the college level was anything but smooth. His first attempt at making West Point's football team was unsuccessful because of his lack of size and his tryout for the baseball team was equally disappointing. Ike was a spray hitter and the Army coach was an advocate of the long ball. Ike was instructed by the coach to work on developing some power and try out again the following spring.

When football practice began in the late summer of 1912, Ike had gained 25 pounds and he was in prime condition due to a distance running and exercise regimen he had followed. When he was trotting off the field in his ill-fitting gear after one of the year's first scrimmages, Army's coach, Ernest Graves, stopped him and told him to report to the team manager and instruct him to outfit him properly–which was Graves' way of letting him know he had made the varsity. Ike later recalled that moment as one of the most special in his life.

By the time the 1912 season kicked off, Ike's teammates from high school would have been amazed. He had been an end throughout his playing days in Abilene but he was now a halfback for one of the top collegiate football programs in the country. *The New York Times* said this about him: "He's one of the most promising backs in Eastern football."

Army won three of its first four games that season and then began earnest preparation for contest number five against the Carlisle Indian Institute, a match-up many were expecting to be football's game of the year.

Carlisle was coached by Glenn "Pop" Warner, one of the most successful coaches in college football history and were led on the field by Jim Thorpe, who had captured the attention of the world a few months before with his unforgettable performance in the 1912 Olympics in Stockholm, when he won the Decathlon and the Pentathlon. Carlisle was undefeated thus far in the season. It was widely believed if they got by Army they would be a virtual shoo-in to be the number-one team in the country when the season ended.

The contest had a number of interesting angles besides Carlisle's quest for the top ranking. It matched a team of future Army officers, representing the sons of Custer, and all the other Indian fighters the academy had produced that had been hand-picked by senators and congressmen, against a team of the sons of braves and warrior chiefs who had been recruited by Indian agents throughout the West.

The style of play of the two teams was as different as their backgrounds. Army relied on size, power, and a stonewall defense while Carlisle relied on speed, quickness, and a razzle-dazzle offense.

Ike and Jim Thorpe did share something in common that day. Under the rules enforced at that time, they were both actually ineligible to participate, because they had both earlier played for pay. There was a two-year gap between Ike's graduation from high school and his entering West Point. During this period, he picked up some cash on the diamond with the biggest thing to hit Abilene since the railroad arrived—professional baseball. The town's newspaper and several other businesses had formed the Abilene Baseball Association and secured a franchise in the Central Kansas League.

To keep costs down and allow the smaller cities in the league to be competitive, a salary cap was imposed on the teams. While the league was concerned about player pay, it was apparently not concerned about a player's identity, as Ike and reportedly a number of others played in the league under aliases, in order to protect their current or future eligibility for participation in collegiate sports.

Soon after arriving home from Europe after World War II, Ike was guest of honor of the New York Giants baseball game at the Polo Grounds. Before the contest, reporters overheard him telling Giant Manager Mel Ott about his covert professional baseball career, which he called "one of the dark secrets of my life." Once, after he had left the presidency, Ike was pressed by a reporter for an interview about his summer of professional baseball but he declined, sending word through an aide that the whole matter was too complicated to explain.

Thorpe had also played professional baseball for a team in Rocky Mount, North Carolina, in 1909 and 1910 and with a team in Oklahoma that barnstormed around that state in 1911. Unlike Ike, he had not played under an alias.

In the numerous accounts of Ike's life history, there are a number of differing versions of what actually happened on the field against Carlisle that day. The three most popular versions seem to be, one, that Ike injured his knee tackling Thorpe and never played football again. The second is that Thorpe ran for two touchdowns, passed for another, kicked three field goals and three extra points and had a 90-yard touchdown nullified by a penalty. A third is that Ike and a teammate planned to knock Thorpe out of the game by a hard simultaneously administered tackle with one hitting Thorpe high and one hitting him low. In this account, the tackle is carried out as planned, but Thorpe shows no effects from the vicious hit and runs for a long gain on the next play.

Ike attempted to set the record straight while he was president and issued a statement through his press secretary about the game. He said he and a teammate named Benedict had concocted a plan about a simultaneous hit and had attempted to carry it out but they missed. The attempt did, however, result in two players having to leave the game because of being injured on the play: Ike and Benedict. The two missed their target and collided with each other and they both had their bells rung and had to be taken from the game and did not return.

The account of the game in *The New York Times* makes no note of Ike and Benedict's play, but it does describe a very embarrassing defeat for the Army team. They scored an early first-period touchdown, but after that it was all Thorpe and Carlisle. *The New York Times* reporter described the action in a style some 80 years or so before political correctness, "The redskins ran wild and routed Army 27-6." It was a very physical game and one player from each side was ejected for unnecessary roughness. The Army squad did bang up Thorpe in the second half and he had to lie prone on the field with an injured shoulder for several minutes, but he shook off the injury and stayed in the game. Thorpe, who would finish the season as the nation's leading scorer with 198 points, did not score a touchdown that day, but he did kick three points after touchdowns.

The Carlisle's team quest to finish the season as the best in the nation was abruptly ended the next Saturday when they were upset by an unheralded University of Pennsylvania team, 34-26. Several weeks later, a Springfield, Massachusetts, reporter heard about Thorpe having played professional baseball. He filed a story about it which started the ball rolling and would ultimately lead to Thorpe being stripped of his Olympic medals.

Thorpe went on to play professional football and professional baseball. After his playing career, he fell on hard times and became an alcoholic. For a period of time, he worked at very menial jobs. His life rebounded somewhat after the Los Angeles Olympics of 1932 sparked renewed interest in him and led to an improved economic situation, but he would continue to struggle with alcohol for the remainder of his life.

Like Thorpe, Ike's world was turned upside down shortly after the Carlisle-Army game. In Army's next game against Tufts, he injured his left knee on a running play, which set in motion the events that would end his football career. After the game, Ike was taken to the infirmary. He spent a couple of days there and then was released and told to take it easy. A few days later, he chose to participate in an equestrian drill and as a result suffered a disastrous consequence.

The drill called for the rider to vault from his horse. When Ike executed the move from his mount and his left leg struck the ground, the leg crumpled beneath him. His knee had been injured much more seriously than originally diagnosed and his playing days were over, not only in football but in baseball as well. It would also affect his play in a game he had not taken up yet—golf—as the injury would always make it difficult for him to properly transfer his weight from his right side to the left side on his downswing. This would cut down on his distance and make him susceptible to hitting a slice and, as a result, despite have the best equipment and instruction available, his handicap would always be in the 14 to 18 range.

Given his baseball background, one would have thought Ike would have been eager to take part in one of the game's time-honored traditions. For decades, about the only thing the hapless Washington Senators baseball franchise had going for it was the privilege of hosting the opening day of the baseball season for the American League. The reason: so the President of the United States could throw out the first ball.

President Taft had started the tradition of throwing out the first ball at the Washington team's opener in 1910. Since Taft's first throw, the President's participation in the opening day ceremonies had become a colorful part of the national pastime. Only a few times since then, due to war or other emergencies, had a president not filled this role.

Appalling many baseball fans, Ike had elected to skip the throwing out the first ball tradition in favor of starting his own tradition, an Augusta National one he would enjoy seven out of the eight years he was in the White House.

After World War II, Ike had attended several golf tournaments, but he found his presence created too much of a distraction to the gallery and the golfers. He knew if he were ever present during Masters Week, it would create just too many problems. Since attending the tournament was out, Ike opted for the next best thing: a week-long golf vacation at Augusta National the week after the event, which typically included a round with the winner of that year's Masters. Opening Day for the Washington team was set for the day after Ike's scheduled departure for Augusta. A scheduling snafu already had Ike interrupting his vacation for a quick one-day trip back to Washington the day after the opener to give an address to the American Newspaper Editors Association. And much to the dismay of Major League Baseball, he was not about to give up any more Augusta time. Vice President Nixon was instructed to warm up; he was going to pinch hit for Ike and throw out the first ball.

Ben Hogan won the Masters the day before Ike's arrival with a record-setting score of 14-under par. Ike's goal for this trip was to set a personal record. He was seeking for the first time to break 90 at Augusta National. He didn't come close his first two rounds, the second of which was played with Hogan. After he concluded that round, he received word that rain had forced the postponement of the baseball game back in Washington. Since he was going to be in Washington on the next day anyway to deliver his speech, The American League office had contacted Ike's chief of staff at the White House and asked if Ike could now accommodate them and throw out the first ball. Ike said yes. Before dinner that evening, he wanted to make sure his arm would be ready for his first ball duties, so he and an aide had a brief game of catch behind the Augusta National clubhouse.

The next day Ike's arm was ready but his stomach was not. After his game of catch, he had dined in the Augusta National dining room and soon thereafter developed symptoms of food poisoning.

Despite being in tremendous discomfort, Ike gamely flew to Washington to honor his commitments. During his speech to the American Newspaper Editors Association, he had to cling to the lectern and several times he thought he was about to faint. After the speech, aides found a spot with a couch for Ike to lie down on for a few minutes before he had to leave for the ballpark. At the game, he made the throw and then ducked out of the stadium at the end of the second inning and flew back to Augusta and spent the next two days in bed. On the third day, he was back on the course and accomplished his goal of breaking 90 with an 88. The following day, the last of his stay, he teed it up again and again broke 90, this time with an 86.

3

MAXIMUM GOLF & HIGH POLL NUMBERS

Soon after Ike departed, Augusta National closed down until late October and Ike's golf headquarters shifted to the Burning Tree Golf Club a short distance from the White House in Bethesda, Maryland. Its membership roll was filled with senators, congressmen, Supreme Court justices, and generals and admirals. The club had given Ike an honorary membership shortly after the end of World War II. At this time, the general public had the impression Burning Tree was a plush showplace when actually, it was very unpretentious. It was just a golf club. It had no tennis courts, no swimming pool, and no extravagant dining room. It did not even have a bar, and women, as is still the case today, were not allowed.

The clubhouse was a small building built of gray fieldstone and red brick. Its rug-less wooden floor was heavily scarred by golf shoe spikes. The dining area consisted of two long, 14-place tables serviced by two attendants. Joining Ike on the Burning Tree member roster were the three Republican golfers who had been swept into office with him: Jack Westland, the reigning U.S. Amateur champion; Prescott Bush; and Barry Goldwater. Westland's lengthy competitive amateur career had taken him to country clubs all over the nation. He described Burning Tree as the most informal golf club he had ever seen. This easygoing camaraderie was the reason Ike chose Burning Tree over the more lavish clubs that were available to him. He could grab a quick lunch in the clubhouse, don his golf shirt, play his round, and then come back into the clubhouse for a rubber of bridge before heading back to the White House. The members adopted a special rule in order to accommodate him. No one, under any circumstances, was to start a conversation with him.

Soon after Ike's inauguration, Burning Tree's rigid no-women-on-the-grounds policy placed Prescott Bush in a tough spot. The new Republican senator from Connecticut was given a most unenviable assignment. There was to be a dinner in Ike's honor at the club, hosted by the Republicans in the Senate. Bush was assigned to inform Margaret Chase Smith, the Republican senator from Maine who had been elected to the Senate in 1948, that she would be excluded from the event because of Burning Tree's policy barring women.

Bush protested the assignment and asked the powers that be at Burning Tree to make an exception, but they refused. Bush swallowed hard and proceeded to carry out the mission in a face-to-face meeting. Bush, recalling the meeting years later, said, "She absolutely hit the ceiling...She was simply–furious–furious."

Stung by Smith's blistering reaction to being excluded, Bush went back to the powers that be at Burning Tree and pleaded again for an exception to the rule. Being on the receiving ended of Smith's wrath must have sharpened Bush's persuasive skills. He won the appeal. Delighted with himself, he went back to Smith to tell her the good news. Her reaction left Bush with more persuading to do. She told him, "I wouldn't come now for anything! Nobody could make me go!"

Bush begged for her to be reasonable and then told her he would pick her up and bring her home and that he had already told Ike she would be sitting on his right at the dinner. Bush admitted later the seating arrangements had not yet been discussed with Ike but he felt like he needed to use every means at his disposal to win her over. She finally relented and agreed to come. However, there was a chill in her relationship with Bush and Ike that lasted throughout the time both men were in office.

Burning Tree was built in 1922 by four District of Columbia residents who had become frustrated at the long waits to tee off at courses in and around Washington. The course got its name from a tree that once stood at the highest point of the club's property and that had bright red leaves when it bloomed in the spring. The course was considered to be a fair test of a golfer's ability. It measured slightly over 6,700 yards in length from the back tees and featured fast, postage stamp-size greens. The only water on the course was a brook that was 100 yards off the tee on the 18th hole. The brook was called McIntyre's Brook in honor of Marvin McIntyre, who was a member of Franklin Roosevelt's staff. Club legend has it that one day, after several failed attempts to clear the brook from the tee, McIntyre threw both his clubs and a mocking playing companion into it.

On days Ike was on the course, which were typically Wednesday and Saturday afternoons, the Secret Service agents checked automobiles and occupants at the gate and were amply deployed over the grounds. But the biggest threat to Ike's safety might well have been Ike himself. On the course, he was an eager beaver. After hitting his tee shot, he would practically race to his ball and begin studying his next shot, seemingly oblivious to the fact that his playing companions' balls often lay behind him. This added a good deal of pressure to their next shot with Ike often very close to being in their line of fire.

An invite to play a round with Ike at Burning Tree was a much hoped for request among Washington's circles. One of those anxiously awaiting the call was his Vice President, Richard Nixon. Like Ike, Nixon had played football in college, but that pretty much ends the athletic comparison of the two, and even that shared experience was radically different. Ike was on his way to being a star at West Point until his knee injury ended his football career. Nixon was a scrub on the Whittier College team where he was scrimmage fodder for the first team during practice and then rode the bench on game day. He played end and had a build woefully smaller than his first team counterparts. The Whittier coach believed his players should always go all out and not let up in practice, so Nixon took a pounding each day. But he won the respect of his teammates, for each time they mowed him down, he would get up, dust himself off, and then give it everything he had on the next play, which, unfortunately for him, wasn't much. Nixon's golf game wasn't much, either. He had taken up the game only three years before and had played more out of political necessity than anything else. Soon after Ike's inauguration, there were press reports of Nixon being a frequent patron of a local public driving range, working on his game in anticipation of getting a call from Ike. He did not have to wait too long. The call came in early May that year.

Ike thought Nixon had to be sandbagging his reported 20-handicap and picked him as his partner that day. Nixon's play that day validated he was, at a bare minimum, a 20 handicapper, and he and Ike took a beating. Later, Nixon would write about the occasion and describe how after the round Ike chewed him out like a Dutch uncle saying, "Look here; you're young, you're strong, and you can do a lot better than that!" Shamed into taking up the game seriously, Nixon took lessons and began to play regularly. By Ike's second term, he was playing to a 12 handicap.

Burning Tree was far from being just a GOP enclave. There were just as many Democrats on the membership roster as Republicans. Notables among them: Attorney Clark Clifford, regarded as the epitome of the Washington super-lawyer, he was a key advisor to President Truman and had been the chief architect of Truman's stunning upset victory over Thomas Dewey in the 1948 presidential election; senators and future presidents John F. Kennedy and Lyndon Johnson; and two more powerful members of the Senate body: J. William Fulbright from Arkansas and Stuart Symington from Missouri. Symington was considered one of the best golfers at Burning Tree and both he Fulbright were on occasion part of Ike's foursome.

As it did in countless other facets of American life, the

Great Depression had set golf back on its heels. The game showed signs of at least a partial recovery in the late 1930s through late 1941, only to be clobbered again by World War II. Since the end of the war, golf had been making modest progress but that all changed when Ike took office in 1953. The effects of having an avid golfer in the White House produced a surge in interest in the game across the country.

Fred Cochran, then the promotional director of the Professional Golfers Association, pretty well summed up the feelings of the golf community when he stated he believed, "Ike's infectious enthusiasm was the greatest thing that had ever happened to the game."

Although only just a few were able to witness Ike in action on the course, many residents of and tourists in the nation's capital did get to see him working on his game on the grounds of 1600 Pennsylvania Avenue. Weather permitting, Ike practiced almost daily on the White House's south lawn. Working with his favorite club, the eight-iron, he would hit shots in the direction of the White House fountain and the ornamental pool. During the fall and winter months when the leaves were off the trees, passersby could easily see him. In the spring and summer, the foliage would conceal him, but observant late afternoon residents and tourists could still see ball after ball raining down on the lower part of the White House grounds.

Ike was not the first president to practice golf at the White House. Warren Harding, who was just as passionate about his game as Ike, was the first. The most popular canine to date in the nation's history, Harding's Airedale "Laddie Boy" would retrieve his master's shots. During Ike's years at the White

House, that duty belonged to Sergeant John Moaney. An African-American, Moaney had been assigned as Ike's orderly shortly after Ike arrived in England to lead the Allied forces. After Ike left the Army, his five-star rank afforded him a small staff in retirement and he asked Sergeant Moaney to remain as part of his team. Once Ike reached the White House, Moaney became his valet. In addition to maintaining the Commander-in-Chief's wardrobe, Moaney always kept Ike's golf shoes, golf clubs, and a shag bag full of balls at the ready for a practice session.

Thanks to an evening at the opera during his first spring in office, Ike came into the possession of a high-tech golf device designed to assist a golfer in perfecting his swing. That night at the opera, Ike had a conversation with Lewis Strauss, the chairman of the Atomic Energy Commission. Strauss informed Ike of the device developed by one of the country's top scientific minds. Within a few days one of the prototypes of the machine arrived at the White House for Ike's use and he reportedly worked with it a good deal.

The designer of the device was Luis W. Alvarez, a renowned physics professor at the University of California. Early in World War II, Alvarez had developed a system for submarine hunting aircraft that would deceive enemy radar operators into believing an aircraft was going away from them instead of coming toward them. Soon after that, he created the Ground Controlled Approach system which allowed ground-based operators using special precision displays to guide airplanes in for landings. Alvarez spent the summer of 1943 in England testing the system, landing planes returning from battle in bad weather, and also training Allied personnel in the use of the system.

In the fall of 1943, Alvarez joined the team at Los Alamos, New Mexico, that was working on America's first atomic bombs. His first assignment there was not on the bomb. It was to come up with a means of determining how far along the Germans were in their atomic program. Alvarez recommended planes carrying a system to detect the radioactive gases that a nuclear reactor produces fly over Germany. His plan was implemented. No gases were detected because the German program had not yet been successful in developing an operational nuclear reactor. After that, Alvarez's assignment moved from detection to detonation.

Since the work on Little Boy, the uranium bomb that would be dropped on Hiroshima, was already far along when he arrived at Los Alamos, Alvarez was assigned to the team working on Fat Man, the plutonium bomb that would be used on Nagasaki. It required a much more intricate detonation system than Little Boy, which Alvarez developed.

Although Alvarez did not work on Little Boy, he did get to see it used. The Hiroshima bomb drop mission consisted of three planes: The Enola Gay, which carried Little Boy; The Great Artiste, equipped with instrumentation to measure the effects of the bomb; and Necessary Evil, which carried scientific observers and cameras. Alvarez was one of the scientific observers on Necessary Evil.

After the war, Alvarez returned to his post as a professor at the University of California at Berkeley. In the early 1950s, he began working on a training aid for his favorite recreational pursuit—golf. It was called the stroboscopic golf training device. It used bright flashes of light to illuminate the club position at five points during the downswing. This allowed the user to determine whether the club head was on the proper path to the ball, so tendencies to hit a hook or slice could be corrected. It was also equipped with a timing device that measured the speed of the swing.

Often when out at Burning Tree, Ike's playing partners were his gang members from Augusta. They regularly visited Ike on weekends for golf during the day and bridge sessions in the evening. During the gang's first weekend visits in late May of 1953, Ike took them up to the presidential retreat 60 miles north of the White House in Maryland's Catoctin Mountains. President Roosevelt, at the urging of his doctors, had had the retreat built in 1942. He named the retreat Shangri La. Shortly after Ike took office, he changed the name to Camp David, in honor of his grandson. During that first trip to the retreat by the gang, they traveled over to a nearby nine-hole course for their golf. Although they weren't expecting it to be an Augusta National-type venue, it was far from being in the type of condition they would find enjoyable.

Soon after this weekend, some changes were made to the grounds of Camp David. Its main building, a rustic-type lodge, is perched atop a ridge. At the base of the ridge lay a small clearing approximately 140 yards in length and about the same distance in width. Noted golf course architect Robert Trent Jones was brought in to develop this limited space into a place Ike and his guests could enjoy a little golf.

Robert Trent Jones was no stranger to government projects.

He had essentially gotten his start designing courses for The Works Project Administration (WPA). The WPA was the largest federal government effort to provide employment for unskilled labor during the Great Depression. Along with its principal projects of public buildings and roads were a number of parks and recreational facilities. In this mix were a number of golf courses that gave young Robert Trent Jones his start as a course designer. This got his career rolling and it took off thanks to slow play at Bobby Jones' home club in Atlanta.

After he returned from World War II, Bobby Jones had promised his friends in his hometown of Atlanta he was going to design and build a new golf course there. He knew the project would require an enormous amount of time. As a result it simmered on the back burner for quite a while. Finally, one day he was playing the fifth hole at his home course, East Lake Golf Cub, when he became very frustrated by the slow play of the group in front of him. He paced back and forth and stomped the ground in a huff. Finally, to the surprise of his playing partners, he snatched up his ball and said, "Let's go build that new course." And he walked briskly back to the clubhouse.

Jones picked Robert Trent Jones to assist him in the design for the Peachtree Golf Club in Atlanta. It opened in 1948 and Robert Trent Jones' career skyrocketed soon after. Over the next five decades he would design over 500 golf courses across the United States and in 35 foreign countries.

At the clearing at Camp David, Jones built an Augusta-worthy green with a bunker on its left side. On its right-hand edge he constructed four tees—the first, 100 yards in distance from the green and 15 feet above its level; the second, 140 yards distant, with the tee 20 feet above; the third, 120 yards distant, with the tee 20 feet below the level of the green; and the fourth, 80 yards in length with the tee 15 feet below. On subsequent visits, Ike and the gang spent a great deal of time making use of Robert Trent Jones' handy work.

As the months of his first year in office ticked by, there were concerns in the Ike camp that too much attention on his golf would have a negative impact on his image with the public. For this reason, Cliff Roberts discouraged Ike from accepting a request from the Professional Golf Association to serve as its honorary chairman for National Golf Day, which it sponsored along with *Life* magazine. Roberts also suggested Ike's interest in other sports be played up to offset the golf coverage. But a Gallup Poll in late June proved these concerns were unfounded. When respondents were asked, "In your opinion, do you think President Eisenhower is taking too much time off from his job as President to play golf, or not?" the overall results were:

Yes, he is---17%

    No, he is not---73%

    No opinion---10%

    Breaking down the respondents by political affiliation the numbers were:

    REPUBLICANS

    Yes, he is---10%

    No, he is not---83%

    No opinion---7%

DEMOCRATS

Yes, he is---23%

No, he is not---65%

No opinion---12%

INDEPENDENTS

Yes, he is---13%

No, he is not---76%

No opinion---11%

In mid-August of 1953, as would be their practice for the next several years, Ike and wife Mamie departed Washington for a summer vacation in her hometown of Denver. While there, Ike and Mamie stayed at her mother's home. An office was set up for Ike at nearby Lowery Air Force Base. He worked there in the mornings and then he would golf on most afternoons at the Cherry Hills Country Club. During this stay, Cliff Roberts and a number of other Augusta National members began what would become an annual pilgrimage to Denver to play golf with Ike while he was on his summer break.

After their marriage, one of Ike and Mamie's first residences was at Fort Meade, Maryland. Not long after their arrival, one day while Ike was on duty, Mamie heard a knock on her door. When she opened it, she found the President of the United States, Woodrow Wilson, and Newton Baker, the Secretary of War, standing on her stoop. The two were making an inspection tour of the base and they had decided to make an impromptu stopover at the base housing area to talk with a few Army wives. After a few moments of exchanging pleasantries, Secretary Baker asked Mamie, "What does your husband do best?" Mamie, obviously unnerved by finding the President of the

United States on her doorstep said, "He plays a good hand of poker."

On this particular vacation, Ike shocked the wife of a Colorado rancher just as Wilson had shocked Mamie. Since his boyhood in Abilene, Ike had loved hunting and fishing. One day during this vacation, which was 25 days in length, Ike took a break from golf and he and a longtime friend of Mamie's family, Denver mortgage banker Aksel Nielsen, went up into the Rockies to a property Nielsen owned to do some trout fishing. By noon the two had a combined catch of a dozen good-sized trout. Ike wanted to cook up the catch but was missing some items to make that happen. So he asked to be driven to a nearby ranch house where he knocked on the door and requested from a stunned housewife to "borrow" a slab of bacon, a pound of butter, a large paper bag, corn meal, and salt and pepper. Ike then returned to Nielsen's property and while Nielsen cleaned the fish, Ike built a camp fire and set the bacon to frying in a skillet. While it fried, he put the cornmeal, salt, and pepper in the paper bag, and shook the cleaned fish in it. When a sizeable amount of fat had melted away from the bacon, he added an equal amount of butter to the pan and then placed in the trout. Within minutes he was dishing out a mouthwatering delight to Nielsen, his Secret Service detail, and the small press pool that had accompanied him.

Ike's cooking skills had been developed at an early age. One of his brothers had been gravely ill for an extended period and needed all of Ike's mother's attention. During this crisis, Ike was given the responsibility of preparing the evening meal. His cooking skills were further enhanced a few years later, when he had to drop out of school for a year because he had missed too many days as the result of an injury that almost cost him one of his legs. During this break from formal education, Ike spend many of his days getting an education in hunting and fishing and how to cook what he killed and caught from Bob Davis, an itinerant trapper who frequented the Abilene area.

Earlier in this first year in office, Ike began the practice of hosting what would become called "stag dinners" at the White House on close to a monthly basis. The invitees would be 10 to 12 men with diverse backgrounds, from captains of industry and finance, doctors and lawyers, ranchers, religious leaders, and usually one sports figure such as Ben Hogan or legendary West Point football coach Earl "Red" Blaik.

The informal gathering would begin at about 7:30 with cocktails, followed by dinner. After dinner the group would retire to the White House's Red Room for after-dinner drinks and more conversation. The evening usually wrapped up around 11:00 p.m. Ike used these dinners to get opinions from a cross-section of the country. He also used them to throw out his thoughts and opinions for size. More times than not, there was a member of Augusta National in the mix. For his October 1953 stag dinner, there were three: Cliff Roberts, Ellis Slater, and Bobby Jones.

The year before, at television's Emmy Awards, the first lady of the American stage, Helen Hayes, and Thomas Mitchell, who had played Scarlett O'Hara's father in *Gone With the Wind* and Uncle Billy in *It's a Wonderful Life* won for best dramatic one-time performances by an actress and actor. Lucille Ball won Best Comedy Actress for *I Love Lucy*. Jack Webb's *Dragnet* won for best Mystery Series. Edward R. Murrow's *See It Now* took honors for Best Public Affairs show. Joining this stellar group as television's "Most Outstanding Personality" for that year was a man Bobby Jones greatly admired and wanted to meet. Ike learned of Jones' interest in this individual and invited the Emmy winner to the dinner so his good friend could make his acquaintance. The television star's name was Bishop Fulton J. Sheen.

Prior to becoming a hit on TV, Sheen had been a professor at the Catholic University of America in Washington, D.C., hosted the nationally broadcast Catholic Hour radio program, and had written a number of books.

In the early '50s, NBC's *The Texaco Star Theatre*, Milton Berle's variety show, owned the 8 p.m. time slot on Tuesday night. The DuMont Television Network, which existed from the mid-'40s until the mid-'50s, expected anything it put in this time slot would be killed by Berle's show. So it decided to come up with a low-cost program, just to fill the spot. They came up with a show titled *Life is Worth Living* hosted by Bishop Sheen. The hour-long program had a one-minute commercial at the beginning and a one-minute commercial at its conclusion. The other 58 minutes featured talks by Bishop Sheen on the moral issues of the day. The show became an overnight sensation, regularly pulling in audiences in the budding era of television of over 20 million. Sheen's Emmy would be the only one ever awarded for a DuMont Network show.

At the dinner, Jones and Sheen were seated together at Ike's table. In a letter of appreciation to Ike a few days after that evening, Jones wrote, "I find it difficult to say anything closer to the truth than what I said to you on the steps of the White House; namely, that this was one of the most memorable evenings of my life."

In the early 50s, the Army-Navy football game, played before 100,000 fans and a national television audience in Philadelphia, rivaled today's Super Bowl in grabbing the attention of the nation. Taking most of the White House staff with him, Harry Truman had attended seven of the eight of these contests played during his presidency and everyone expected Ike, a former player for Army, to be in attendance. But like the opening day of baseball season, this major happening on the country's sports calendar, on the Saturday of the Thanksgiving Holiday weekend, was going to take a back seat to golf. Ike was going to Augusta National instead of the game.

On this trip to Augusta, Ike would experience a major upgrade in his accommodations. After Ike won the election, Bobby Jones and Cliff Roberts knew in order for him to continue to enjoy Augusta National as President, Jones' small cabin would no longer be feasible as his quarters for his family members, personal staff, and Secret Service protection. So soon after Ike took office, they solicited donations from approximately 50 members of the club to build a new cabin for him.

Located a short pitch shot from the 10th tee, the new structure was a cabin in name only. It had three floors, including a basement that was used by the Secret Service as its command center. Also, another construction project at the club had been completed. It was an addition to the clubhouse that now housed the club's pro shop. On the addition's upper level, directly above the pro shop, was an office for Ike to use during his stays.

All of the gang was present for the cabin's official unveiling. They golfed with Ike during the day and in the evening they gathered for bridge.

There was one occurrence that put a bit of a damper on an overall very enjoyable holiday. It occurred on Ike and Mamie's first night in the cabin, when that evening a member of his own political party, Joseph McCarthy, United States Senator from Wisconsin, attacked Ike during a nationwide television broadcast for almost a full half hour.

McCarthy believed there were large numbers of Communists and Soviet spies and sympathizers inside the United States federal government and he was on a crusade to clean them out. This was not the first time McCarthy had taken a swipe at Ike. Back in the spring, Ike had nominated Charles "Skip" Bohlen, a career diplomatic and a golf partner of his in Paris while he was leading NATO, to be ambassador to the Soviet Union. McCarthy tried to block the nomination, contending Bohlen was a Communist appeaser. McCarthy was unsuccessful, but he did delay the nomination, causing some political pain for Ike.

A few days before Ike had departed Washington for his Thanksgiving vacation at Augusta, former President Harry Truman had attacked McCarthy and his crusade during a television interview. McCarthy demanded and was granted thirty minutes of television air time to respond to Truman's attack. His response was aired as Ike and Mamie were settling in for their first night in the new cabin. McCarthy spent the first five minutes of the broadcast attacking Truman. Then he gave Ike a cabin-warming gift, by using the remaining 25 minutes to accuse him and his administration of coddling of Communists.

A number of Ike's aides and advisors urged him to go after McCarthy but he resisted stating, he did not want to get into a pissing contest with a skunk.

4

HOGAN, ALIENS, & MCCARTHY

Ike awoke on New Year's Day in 1954 in the Eisenhower Cabin at Augusta National, having arrived there on Christmas Day for a 10-day stay. A short time later, he likely extracted a small amount of pleasure from the fact that the White House press corps, with many of its group in a hungover state, were obliged to crawl out of bed and report on his opening drive of the year. Soon after Ike returned to Washington, a flap developed over an article in *Collier's* magazine about the Eisenhower Cabin.

After Ike's Thanksgiving stay, Jones and Roberts had allowed members of the press to tour the cabin under the condition they would not print specific details about its layout for security reasons. *Collier's* had been one of the country's leading weekly publications for over sixty years but its circulation was dropping and it had recently been forced to cut back to publishing bi-weekly.

Although in their January 22, 1954 issue, *Collier's* had an editorial backing the idea that a president needed such a getaway, the issue also contained an article titled "Mamie's Cabin." Perhaps under the pressure to boost its declining circulation, they opted to ignore the ground rules laid down by Jones and Roberts that had allowed their magazine access. The story went so far as to have an artist draw a cutaway interpretation that showed and identified practically every room in the structure. These details and the adjectives the story used to embellish its descriptions of the cabin's furnishings and decor infuriated Bobby Jones. So he fired off this letter to *Collier's* publisher, Edward Anthony:

January 15, 1954

Mr. Edward Anthony, Publisher
    Collier's
    640 Fifth Avenue
    New York 19, N. Y.

Dear Mr. Anthony:

In view of the friendly and understanding tone of the editorial on page 110 of the January 22nd *Collier's*, it is exceedingly difficult for me to understand how you could have permitted the publication in the same issue of the article on "Mamie's

Cabin." If you recognize, as you say you do, the right, and even absolute need, of the President to have some relaxation at his favorite game, I cannot understand how you could approve an article which so exaggerates and distorts the efforts of a few of his friends to make it possible for him to enjoy his favorite retreat.

The Augusta National Golf Club objects strongly to the story on two major counts:

One, because of the publication of the purported floor plan of the house, which while it is not entirely accurate, is close enough to provide unnecessarily dangerous information to an ill-intentioned person. This was done, according to my information, despite the fact that you were personally informed by two of our members that the people charged with protecting the President's safety have repeatedly requested us not to release this kind of information.

Two, because apparently the whole intention of the article was to exaggerate the so called "sumptuousness" and extravagance of the house. In this connection it should be stated that there are many statements in the article that are contrary to fact and that each one of these misstatements contributes to the overall impression I have mentioned.

Perhaps it may be helpful if I remind you that the President was a member of the Augusta National long before he became a candidate for the Presidency. During this time he was in the habit of spending vacations there with his entire immediate family, including his son's family, and Mrs. Eisenhower's mother. A party of this size, which sometimes included his physician and others, required most all of the cabins on the Club grounds.

When General Eisenhower became President Eisenhower, a number of our members grew concerned that under these altered circumstances it would not be possible for the President to enjoy the Augusta National, because we all knew that he would never be willing to place upon the Club the additional burdens which his visits as President would entail. It was then that the idea of this house came into being, and we decided to provide it, both as a gesture of appreciation to the man for undertaking this great service to his country, as well as to provide additional facilities which were badly needed by the Club itself. The house therefore was designed so that it could not only accommodate the Eisenhower family, but could also be separated into units for the general use of other members when the President might not be occupying it.

The Augusta National Golf Club has tried very hard to maintain the atmosphere of privacy and informality which all of us feel is so important to the President's enjoyment of the place. We have also tried very hard to avoid the slightest suspicion that the Club might be seeking publicity or other advantage from the fact that one of its members has been elected President. We earnestly believe that we are entitled to cooperation from publications such as *Collier's* in both of these aims.

It is of course true that the house is a nice house of first class and up-to-date construction. It is also true that the budget for furnishing the house was by no means a liberal one, and it is certainly true that there are many homes in Augusta that are far more "sumptuously" appointed.

It is obvious, of course, that nothing can undo the damage that has already been done by this article. I do hope very much, however, that I may have your assurance that we have seen the end of this sort of publicity, at least insofar as your magazine is concerned.

Very truly yours,

Robert T. Jones, Jr., President

Augusta National Golf Club

Whereas in February 1953, Ike had taken a short golf vacation at Augusta National, he likely decided Augusta might be a little over-exposed, so for a February golf break in 1954, he opted instead to go to Palm Springs, California, and play at the Tamarisk Country Club. This club was home to many high-profile celebrities: Jack Benny, George Burns, Danny Kaye, and the Marx Brothers, just to name a few. The club's professional was none other than Ben Hogan and he played with Ike for his first round of his stay.

During that round with Hogan, a good-sized crowd had gathered around the ninth green near the clubhouse to watch the famous duo complete their front nine. This gathering was witness to quite a golf shot, not from Hogan, but from Ike. On that par-four hole, Ike was laying two and still had approximately 100 yards left to reach the green. To complicate matters, there was a palm tree directly between his ball and the green. With his next swing, Ike sent his ball over the palm tree and dead on target. Within a few seconds, the crowd erupted with cheers and applause as Ike's ball struck the flagstick and dropped down within 12 inches of the cup for a tap-in par.

After that shot, the trip went downhill. Back in Washington, Ike's appointment of California Governor Earl Warren to be Chief Justice of the Supreme Court was being held up by North Dakota Senator William Langer, a fellow Republican who had an axe to grind with Ike over several federal appointments in his state that were made without consulting him. And Senator McCarthy was on another rampage in his hunt for Communists. During a Senate hearing, he had torn into General Ralph Zwicker, who had been decorated for heroism for his actions during the Battle of the Bulge, comparing the General's intelligence to that of a "five-year-old child," and declaring he was "not fit to wear the uniform of a General."

To further spoil the trip, one night at dinner, Ike took a bite of a fried chicken leg and knocked off a cap on one of his front teeth. A local dentist was contacted to fix the problem and Ike was whisked away to his office.

Ike's press secretary was at a cookout and unavailable to explain what was going on. The reporters for the country's two leading wire services, United Press International and the Associated Press, then took to the wire to report their interpretation of what was happening. U.P.I. reported Ike was undergoing 'medical treatment.' The A.P. went a little further. They reported Ike was dead but then retracted the story several minutes later.

Six decades later, stories still whirl about the events of that evening among UFO enthusiasts. They believe Ike's trip to the dentist was a cover story to conceal the fact he had slipped away to Muroc Air Force Base (now Edwards Air Force Base). While at the base, Ike either viewed the bodies of dead aliens and the wreckage of their craft, or met with live aliens who were on a diplomatic mission to Earth.

This year there was no conflict between the American League's opener in Washington and Ike's Augusta plans and he smoothed the feathers of the baseball fans he had ruffled the previous year by making it known well in advance he would be in attendance. The Washington squad played host to the New York Yankees. The game went 10 innings. In the bottom half of the 10th frame, Senators' Mickey Vernon stroked a home run over the right field wall with a man on to give the home team a 5-3 win. Ike was there for every pitch and even hung around to shake Vernon's hand when the game was over.

Ike arrived in Augusta the day after the 1954 Masters had concluded. The tournament had been one of the greatest shows in the history of the event. Sam Snead and Ben Hogan ended up tied after the 72 holes of regulation play and then Snead claimed his final green jacket the next day in an 18-hole playoff.

What made this Masters so special was the performance of Billy Joe Patton, a young amateur from Morganton, North Carolina. From all the players in that year's field, Patton was the least qualified to be there. His invitation had come as a result of Bobby Jones' desire to have a strong amateur presence in the field. When that year's invitations were being considered, Cliff Roberts had asked Bobby Jones if he wanted to invite the Walker Cup team, the group of highly talented amateur golfers selected to represent the U.S. in matches contested biennially, similar to the Ryder Cup, against a team of amateurs from Great

Britain and Ireland. Jones told Roberts he did want the Walker Cup team invited. In a follow-up to Jones' response, Roberts asked whether the invite should go out to the alternates on that squad, and again Jones said yes. Billy Joe Patton was one of the alternates.

Billy Joe's trademark was an incredibly fast swing. He was a streaky golfer. When he was hot, he was unbelievably good and when he was cold you would consider him just your usual above-average local club player. From his first swing in the first round, Billy Joe was hot, incredibly hot, and for the next four days, he was not only the talk of golf, he was the talk of the entire sports world. He was near the lead or in the lead for the entire event. In the final round, he put on quite a show for the huge gallery following him. At the par three sixth, he made a hole-in-one and it appeared he was poised to win the tournament until he reached a hole on the back nine in the final round that has been the undoing of many a Masters' contender.

The thirteenth hole at Augusta is a tempting par five, tempting because with good drive and a good lie in the fairway, a player can reach the green in two for a possible eagle or a two-putt birdie. The down side of going for the green in two is the creek that winds by its front. Many Masters champion hopefuls have seen their chances washed away when their second shots landed in it.

Ike constantly fell victim to the 13th hole's temptation as his caddie, Cemetery, once described in a magazine interview. Cemetery always wanted Ike to lay up with his second shot to avoid the dangers of the creek. He would pull a short-iron out of the bag and try to hand it to Ike, but Ike would say, "No! No!

Give me the wood." The majority of the time, the shot with the wood ended up in the creek. It was after those kinds of shots that Cemetery said Ike developed a case of the red neck, as the veins on the back of his neck would be bulging and fire-engine red.

When Patton reached the 13th tee in the final round of the '54 Masters, he was tied with Snead and Hogan for the lead. He hit a good drive and when he pulled out a wood to go for the green with his second shot, the huge throng following him gave out a tremendous cheer. A few moments later those cheers turned to groans. Patton's shot did not come off the clubface with the zip it needed and fell short into the creek. After taking a penalty stroke and dropping behind the creek, Patton's next shot barely cleared the creek and it took three more shots for him to get the ball into the hole for a disastrous double-bogey seven. He would end the day just one stroke away from joining Snead and Hogan in their playoff.

Since television coverage of the Masters was still a few years away, Cliff Roberts updated Ike at the White House almost hourly on the action taking place in the tournament. Ike was struck by Patton's incredible showing and sent word he would like to play a round with him when he arrived in Augusta. Naturally, Patton was thrilled with the invitation, but it meant he would have to do a good bit of driving. He made his living as a lumber salesman back in North Carolina. Having already missed a week's work playing in the Masters, he was concerned about how things were going back at his job. So he decided to drive the 200 miles back to Morganton to check on things at the office. When he found everything was in order, he drove back to Augusta the next day to play his round with Ike.

Later that same week at Augusta, Ike teed it up with another pretty strong amateur player, this one from the state of Washington: his brother Edgar.

There were six sons born to Ike's parents. The oldest was Arthur. He became a banker in Kansas City. Then came Edgar who, after receiving a law degree from the University of Michigan, set up a practice in Tacoma, Washington. Ike was next. He was followed by Roy, who became a druggist in Junction City, Kansas. Next was Earl, who became an electrical engineer and settled in Pennsylvania. Then came Milton, an educator who served as President of Kansas State University, Penn State, and Johns Hopkins University. Paul, the sixth and youngest brother, died in infancy.

Ike and Edgar had pushed sibling rivalry to its limits when they were growing up. Edgar, a year older than Ike, always liked to say he and Ike would fight for the sheer joy of slugging each other. Ike lived in Edgar's shadow while they were growing up in Abilene. During World War II, Edgar was pressed by reporters to provide information about his now-famous brother's childhood. He wrote Ike asking him if there were any special remembrances he would like to include. Ike wrote back he really didn't have the time to respond at length and then stated:

You could run faster, hit better, field better, tote the football better, and do everything except beat me at shotgun shooting...so it looks to me that if you have to tell them stories about our boyhood, you will have to tell them that I was just the tail to your kite.

Edgar's domination of Ike would also hold true on the golf course as he possessed a single-digit handicap. He played in Bing Crosby's Pro-Am at Pebble Beach and would win four Washington State Senior Titles.

Like Ike, Edgar was in his mid-thirties before he took up golf. He and an associate from his firm decided to take up the game together and play during the middle of the week, when the courses would have less traffic. Unlike Ike, whose Augusta National trip some twenty years after his first round turned him into a golf fanatic, Edgar was hooked from the get-go. Despite his new addiction, his law practice continued to thrive and he became one of the top corporate attorneys in the western United States.

After Ike became president, he and Edgar would slug it out politically with the same fervor they once had with their fists. Edgar was a staunch conservative and would not hold back any punches when he felt his brother's actions were too moderate, which was often. Ike's nomination of Earl Warren to the Supreme Court almost caused Edgar to implode. On the other hand, Ike had to be more than a little upset when it got into print Edgar had said Ike was a little bit socialistic and that he, Edgar, was the only real Republican in the Eisenhower family.

Three weeks after Ike returned from Augusta, it was announced that his ability to practice his game at the White House was going to be significantly enhanced. The United States Golf Association was donating a putting green for its grounds. The USGA would oversee the construction of the 3,000-square-foot green. The turf for the White House green, which would also feature a practice bunker, was transplanted from Aronomink Golf Club, near Philadelphia.

In 1959, one of the most talked about films to hit the motion picture screen was *Anatomy of a Murder*, a courtroom crime drama starring Jimmy Stewart and Lee Remick. It was one of the first mainstream Hollywood films to address sex and rape in graphic terms. For the time, the language in the film was startling to many movie-goers. So startling in fact that the Chicago Police Commissioner and the city's mayor, Richard J. Daley, had it banned in the Windy City. The film's producer and director, the legendary Otto Preminger, went to federal court to fight the ban. The court found the language in the film was realistic and appropriate within the context of the movie's plot and overturned the ban.

The judge in the film was played by a real-life lawyer by the name of Joseph N. Welch, who was making his motion-picture debut. The 69-year-old graduate of Harvard Law School turned in a stellar performance. He also gained a small footnote in motion picture history for being the first actor to say the word "panties" in a film. For his performance, Welch was nominated for a Golden Globe Award for Best Supporting Actor in a Motion Picture.

Four years earlier, on June 9, 1954, Welch had turned in a performance on Capitol Hill that was hands-down the real-life equivalent of Oscar-winning and in the process alleviated what had been one of the biggest headaches for Ike and his administration: Senator Joseph McCarthy.

During Ike's stay in Palm Springs, McCarthy had been fiercely attacking the United States Army for coddling Communists. The Army counter-attacked, charging that McCarthy's office had sought preferential treatment for a staffer who had recently been drafted into the Army. Senate hearings that would become known as the Army-McCarthy hearings were scheduled for late April to look into both sides' allegations.

A little more than a month before the hearings were to begin, Edward R. Murrow staggered McCarthy when he lashed out against him and his tactics on his *See It Now* news program on CBS. Murrow kept the heat on McCarthy for the next several weeks and it noticeably put McCarthy back on his heels.

When the Army-McCarthy hearings got underway the public's interest was very high. So much so that ABC television broadcast the proceeding from gavel to gavel for the next six weeks.

Where Murrow had staggered McCarthy, these hearing finished him off. McCarthy had basked in the glow of the media for almost four years, but now he was losing steam each day the hearings were telecasts. The public had seen unflattering film clips of the senator in action on Murrow's show. During these televised hearings, they were given the opportunity to see McCarthy live in action and by no means were his daily performances on camera a positive for him or his cause.

Although the hearings would last for another week, their emotional climax came on the afternoon of Wednesday, June 9, 1954, while Ike was playing his regular mid-week round at Burning Tree. It was an exchange between McCarthy and

Joseph Welch, who had been retained by the Army to be their lead counsel in the hearings.

This exchange, which has been replayed countless times in documentaries concerning the '50s, the Cold War, and McCarthy, was triggered when McCarthy charged that a young attorney in Welch's Boston firm harbored Communist sympathies.

Welch responded with a righteous outburst that hit all the right buttons. When McCarthy attempted to strike back, Welch cut him off and at which point the large gallery present erupted in ringing applause. From that moment forward, McCarthy ceased to be either a force on the country's political scene or an impediment to Ike's golf game.

A few weeks later, over the Fourth of July holiday, Ike entertained gang members Bill Robinson, Ellis Slater, and Pete Jones and their wives at Camp David. There was plenty of bridge playing and the men spent a lot of time working on their short games on the new Robert Trent Jones layout. During these sessions, wagering was done on the following basis: From the short tee, one had to land the ball on the green and from the three longer tees one had to have the ball come to rest on the green.

Many Democrats thought Ike's frequent golf now presented an opportunity for them to chip away at his popularity. In the summer of 1954, a popular bumper stick displayed by many of their number read: "If we wanted a golfer in the White House, we should have elected Ben Hogan president." The man on point to respond to such taunts was Richard Nixon. He often brought up Ike's golf in speeches and responded to this particular zinger from the Democrats by bringing up the poker playing of Ike's Democratic predecessor Harry Truman with this retort, "If Ike played as much golf as Harry Truman played poker when he was in the White House, Ike would be able to beat Ben Hogan."

These jabs between the two parties were considered typical political small-arms fire but late in this summer the head of the Democratic Party decided to roll out a cannon and fire a shell at Bobby Jones' and Ike's friendship.

In the opening round of the U.S. Open in 1925 at Worcester Country Club in Worcester, Massachusetts, Jones hit his approach shot into the rough on the left side of the green on the par-three 11th. When Jones nestled his club into the tall grass behind the ball for his pitch to the green, the ball moved ever so slightly. No one saw the ball move; not an official, nor Jones' caddie or his playing partner that day, Walter Hagen.

Jones immediately stepped away from the ball and called a one-stroke penalty on himself. He pitched onto the green and two-putted for a double-bogey five. When the fourth and final round concluded, Jones was in a tie for first place with Willie McFarland. The two squared off in a 36-hole playoff for the championship the next day, which Jones lost by one stroke.

If Jones hadn't called the penalty on himself, there wouldn't have been a playoff and he would have won five U.S. Open titles instead of four. Later, Jones was asked about that self-imposed penalty in an interview. He bristled at the notion he had done anything extraordinary by calling the penalty on himself and stated, "You might as well praise me for not robbing banks." Jones was still several years away from his climatic Grand Slam year of 1930 but his act at the 1925 Open firmly established in the public's eye that Bobby Jones was a man of unquestionable integrity.

Over the next almost three decades, Jones' stature continued to soar. So it is not surprising jaws dropped to the floor when, during an appearance before a gathering of the American Bar Association, Stephen Mitchell, the National Chairman of the Democratic Party, was asked to cite an example of corruption in the Eisenhower Administration. In his answer, Mitchell implied a utility company [the Southern Company], which Jones served on the board of directors, was in line to receive a federal contract as a result of Jones' close personal ties with Ike.

Needless to say, Mitchell's insinuation made both Jones and Ike livid. In his response to Mitchell's charge, Jones said:

I resent any implication that the President would be susceptible to such an influence, and I resent the implication that I would be foolish enough to try to bring such influence to bear...it would come as a surprise to me if he had ever known I was a director of the [Southern] Company.

Mitchell could produce no evidence for his charges but he did produce a substantial amount of wrath from Republicans and many fellow Democrats. *The New York Times* took Mitchell to task on its editorial page, calling his attack on Jones a "blunder."

In the last week of August, Congress adjourned for its summer vacation and Ike headed to Denver for a seven-week working vacation. This trip, for the most part, followed the pattern from the previous year. He and Mamie stayed at his mother-in-law's home. He would work mornings at his office at Lowery and played golf at Cherry Hills in the afternoon. And a number of the Augusta National gang came out to play golf with him, a couple making more than one trip. Ike did break from this routine several times to go up into the Rockies for some more trout fishing. On one of these occasions, he got a little prickly with the press corps when one of its members pointed out the fact his catch of 25 was well over the legal limit of 15.

A few weeks after his return to Washington, Ike found himself in the rough politically. When he had won his landslide victory in 1952, on his coattails, Republicans, who had been in the minority by 36 in the House of Representatives, took control by eight seats. In the United States Senate, where they had been the minority by two, Republicans squeaked into control by one seat. Without Ike on the ticket, the pendulum swung in the Democrats' favor and they regained control of the House by twenty-nine seats and the Senate by two seats. Many blamed the damage done to the Republicans' image by Joseph McCarthy for the shift in power. It would be 1980 before Republicans would take control of the Senate again and 1994 before they would be the majority in the House.

Later that month, Ike again took a pass on attending the Army-Navy game in Philadelphia and instead took off for Augusta to gather with his family and the gang for the Thanksgiving Holiday. This trip was the inaugural flight for his new airplane, the Columbine III. It was a Super Constellation built by Lockheed. It replaced the Columbine II, a 1948 Constellation that had served as Ike's plane since he took office.

This new version of the Constellation featured increased stability. Ike could have benefited from having his stability on the ground increased as well, as he would soon begin encountering some very rough going.

5

A HOME AT LAST

Ike returned to Augusta National on Christmas Eve and departed on January 2, 1955. While there he spent a good deal of his time working on his annual State of the Union Address in his office above the pro shop.

On January 7th, Ike delivered his State of the Union Address to Congress and a nationwide television audience at 1:00 p.m. Shortly before 2:00 p.m., he concluded his remarks on the condition and needs of the country and quickly made his way out of the Capitol Building with Mamie to his waiting limousine and sped away to the White House. At the White House, only Mamie exited the limo. It then sped away for Burning Tree Golf Club. Despite the fact there was a light rain falling, Ike wanted to get in a quick nine holes before dark.

A few weeks later, Ike received a group of visitors at the White House. One of them was a labor leader who said to Ike, "You know we are keeping track of the number of times you play golf." Ike told the man to go ahead and that he planned to increase the amount of golf he was playing.

On the last weekend in January, Cliff Roberts came down from New York City to Washington, where he boarded the Columbine III and flew with Ike to Augusta for the weekend.

A few days later, Ike defeated the reigning United States Open champion Ed Furgol, not on the course, but in the balloting for the William D. Richardson Trophy, awarded annually by the Golf Writers Association of America to the individual its members believed had made the most outstanding contribution to the game of golf in the previous year. Ike, who had finished in the runner-up spot in the balloting the year before to Babe Didrickson Zaharias, received 394 votes in the balloting. Furgol took second with 321 votes.

In the United States Golf Association's eyes, Ike's passion for the game was one of the best things that had ever happened to the sport. Ike did, however, shake the ruling body of golf in this country to its core just a few days after receiving the Richardson Award when there were press reports he was using a juiced-up illegal ball. The ball, which had been developed by an Air Force colonel, outdistanced legal balls (those that had been tested and approved by the USGA) by 25 to 30 yards. If these reports were true, the effects of the nation's most celebrated golfer not adhering to the USGA's rules would be devastating to the game. Charles B. Grace, the Chairman of the USGA's Ball and Implement Committee, fired off a letter to Ike at the White House expressing the USGA's serious concerns on the matter.

Ike soon alleviated the USGA's fears when he wrote back to

Mr. Grace within in a week and advised him that he had never used a non-regulation ball.

Ike's golf balls, as well as his golf clubs, were supplied by Bobby Jones. Soon after his retirement from competitive golf and in addition to his practice of law, Jones had signed on with the sporting goods giant Spalding to produce a line of golf clubs bearing his name. He supplied Ike with the newest edition of his clubs as soon as they became available, as well as a never-ending supply of golf balls from Spalding bearing the imprint "Mr. President."

The souped-up golf balls the USGA had been concerned about had been dropped off at the White House by their inventor, and it is unlikely they were the only ones arriving there that day. As soon as Ike took up residence in the White House, golf balls arrived regularly for him in the mail from well-wishers as well as other golf products and tips on how he could improve his game.

The golf balls that arrived at the White House were given to Sergeant Moaney. Periodically, Ike would inspect Moaney's cache of balls and pick out the ones he deemed worthy of being placed in his shag bag and used for practice on the South Lawn and the remainder would be given away.

As spring approached in 1955, an issue with the White House practice green would stir up protests from animal lovers and give his political opponents plenty of fodder to get in some digs at Ike and his golf. The member of Ike's team who would be on the front lines of this row would be James Hagerty, his press secretary. Hagerty was the son of a *New York Times* political correspondent. He was a graduate of Columbia University and he had started his career as a correspondent for the *Times*. One of his first big assignments was covering the campaign of Republican Wendell Willkie against Franklin Roosevelt in 1940. Hagerty became close to Willkie, having drinks and playing golf with him. He concluded after that election season was over that he had seen firsthand how not to run a presidential campaign.

A short time later, Hagerty signed on as press secretary to Thomas E. Dewey, the Republican governor of New York. This would allow him to observe how not to run a presidential campaign two more times, as Dewey lost in 1944 to Franklin Roosevelt, and to Harry Truman in 1948. A few days after Ike won the Republican nomination, Dewey, now serving his third term as New York's governor, loaned Hagerty to Ike to serve as his press secretary during the campaign.

After the election, Hagerty agreed to stay on as Ike's press secretary at the White House. One morning during Ike's post-election stay at Augusta National, the president-elect appeared at the door of the room Hagerty was using as an office and asked him to play golf with him. Hagerty tried to beg off, but Ike insisted. In the golf cart that day between shots, the two worked out the finer details of their working relationship that would last through both of Ike's terms in office.

Hagerty had a very keen political sense and he proved to be very adept at protecting Ike's image and popularity. He transferred the blame for mistakes to government agencies and appropriated credit for achievements to the White House. He was a master at timing the release of big and favorable stories to blanket unfavorable news. On Ike's prolonged golf vacations, he would take along executive orders, appointments, reports, and cost-of-living surveys and would ration them out day by day to make news. His goal was to keep Ike's golf playing far down in the stories about his activities on any given day.

Ike displayed his dependency on Hagerty openly, as he often checked with him during a press conference before he answered a question. Hagerty did not hesitate to appear swiftly at Ike's side while he was answering a question, if he felt his boss was in trouble. At other times, Ike would tell reporters Hagerty would explain a particular point to them after the press conference.

Ike also depended on Hagerty to be a member of his golf foursome whenever there was a spot that needed to be filled. This was usually when the opportunity for a spur-of-the-moment round developed, or on vacation when members of the gang had not yet arrived. Hagerty almost always wore a New York Yankees baseball cap when he played, which was appropriate because he approached hitting the golf ball as if it were a baseball. He used an extremely closed stance and took a Pete Rose-like crouch over the ball. From that position, he would snatch the club back and then, with a convulsive start, lash down at the ball. This swing produced mixed results. His wood shots off the tee went nowhere. They were so bad that when Ike would hit poor drives himself, he would often say ruefully, "Well, there's a Jim Hagerty for you."

But the bespectacled press secretary's extreme weakness off the tee was made up for by the fact that his swing produced surprisingly good shots with his irons, especially his long irons. This part of his game allowed Hagerty to stay fairly competitive with Ike on the course, as he typically shot between 90 and 100.

One of Hagerty's most challenging periods as Ike's press secretary came in the late spring of 1955, when one of his boss' most favorite pieces of government property came under attack —the barely one-year-old White House putting green. This smooth green treasure was Ike's pride and joy and he took great interest in its care and maintenance. So naturally, he went ballistic when he discovered it had come under attack by some furry friends of the previous occupant of that residence–Harry Truman.

Truman liked to take meals on the White House's South Porch and would feed the squirrels who often dropped by to visit him. He also enlisted the aid of a five-year-old boy, whom he appointed as the Official Feeder. There were no such handouts available in the Eisenhower Administration, but the squirrels did find something in the change in presidents that they liked, which was the velvet-like surface of the putting green. It was just perfect for burrowing holes. When Ike first observed the damage the squirrels had done, his legendary fiery temper took over, and he ordered Sergeant Moaney to shoot the squirrels. Cooler heads on the White House staff, who thought gunfire and bloodshed on the grounds of 1600 Pennsylvania Avenue was not the way to go, prevailed. Alternate plans were developed and what was hoped would be a secret White House operation commenced.

An electronics expert was brought in first. He tried high-pitched sounds to drive off the squirrels, but they were obviously used to the high-pitched sounds of Washington and this effort had no effect. Recordings of cat and dog sounds were then tried, but the squirrels weren't rattled. The decision was then made to trap the squirrels and relocate them to areas far away from the White House putting green.

After several squirrels had been trapped and carted off, there was a leak, and the press was made aware of the operation and reported on it. Democrats in Congress seized the moment and began lampooning Ike. The timing could not have been worse, as the coverage of the story reached its peak during National Wildlife Week. Democratic Senator Richard Neuberger of Oregon was the most vocal in the defense of the squirrels. He proposed that a fence be built around the green and began taking donations for that purpose.

Several days later, at a press briefing, Hagerty announced the trapping operation had been stopped and it had resulted in the removal of only three squirrels. Two were taken to the city's Rock Creek Park, and the whereabouts of the third could not be specifically pinned down. Hagerty would only say he had been released somewhere in Northern Virginia. Hagerty contended Ike had not ordered the trapping. He said the president had noticed the squirrel-tampering on the green but did not say anything about trapping the creatures. It was members of the staff who had sought to put things right. He did not, however, know who specifically had come up with the trapping idea.

The Democrats got in one last salvo. They charged District of Columbia laws that protected the squirrels had been broken, and they wanted to know who was going to pay the fine. Hagerty appeared to be thrown off guard when that question was posed to him in a press briefing, but aides quickly came to his rescue, pointing out the fact the White House and its grounds were a National Park and therefore under federal, not local, jurisdiction.

Soon after the squirrel controversy the focus shifted from the White House property to a large house under renovation on a 189-acre farm 60 miles away in Gettysburg, Pennsylvania. Mamie and Ike were soon going to do something they had not previously done in their almost 39 years of marriage: spend the night in a house they actually owned. They had in fact bought this property for their retirement home soon after Ike became president of Columbia University. But Ike's taking command of NATO and then his run for the presidency had kept the improvements the property needed on hold. Soon after Ike took office, the renovation got underway and now it was just about complete. Mamie was very particular about the house's construction and its décor, to the point an exasperated Ike is said to have told a contractor, "For God's sake, just give her what she wants and send me the bill."

When Mamie married Ike in 1916, her affluent upbringing in Denver had left her devoid of the most rudimentary domestic skills. The transition to the lifestyle and income level a young Army officer dictated was quite an adjustment. For the first few years of their marriage, Ike handled a good many of the domestic chores, including the cooking.

In due time, Mamie overcame her domestic shortcomings and over the course of Ike's long military career she became the consummate Army wife. During that time she lived in 18 different quarters from Panama to the Philippines and from the red clay of Georgia to the evergreen forests of Washington

State. She learned to clean, decorate, and move out, and then to clean and decorate again.

Ike and Mamie had bought the farm at the urging of a close friend of Ike's, a man he called his favorite Democrat and one his Augusta National pals had to learn to accept: George E. Allen.

Ike had first met Allen during World War II in London when Allen came over on a mission to assist the Red Cross and the two developed a strong friendship. So strong, on Ike's first trip to Augusta in 1948, he had brought Allen along with him.

A former secretary of the National Democratic Party, Allen, known for his girth and wit, had been a confidant of and regular poker player with both President Franklin Roosevelt and President Harry Truman. In 1950, he had penned a book about his experiences with those two men titled *Presidents Who Have Known Me*.

Allen hailed from Boonville, Mississippi. He had received a law degree from Cumberland College in Lebanon, Tennessee. But practicing law proved not a good fit for him. His portly appearance and irrepressible sense of humor did not serve him well, nor did his lack of attention to detail. Allen liked to tell a story he believed epitomized his legal career. Once he was in court and a judge told an indigent defendant he could pick Allen or another lawyer to represent him. Allen was present in the courtroom, but the other lawyer had yet to arrive. The defendant looked at Allen and then told the judge, "I'll take the other guy."

Allen's law career ended when he entered the Army during World War I. He was soon shipped over to the action and served as a first lieutenant in a machine gun company in France. After the war, he began managing hotels. After a lengthy stint in Chicago, he moved to Washington and became manager of one of the premier hotels in the city. He wasted no time in making many friends in the capital's inner circle. In just four years, he was appointed by Congress to be a District of Columbia Commissioner, which at that time was the equivalent of being one-third mayor and he was soon a regular at President Roosevelt's poker table at the White House.

At the height of the Depression, FDR's right-hand man, Harry Hopkins, asked Allen to be his aide in the Energy Relief Administration. Later, Allen became a vice president of the Home Insurance Company. He was soon making more connections and receiving appointments to the boards of several large corporations. In 1943, he became secretary of the Democratic Party. In 1944, he was one of the early backers of Harry Truman as FDR's running mate.

When Truman became president, Allen had a regular seat at his poker table. Truman eventually appointed him to be the director of the Reconstruction Finance Corporation, the agency also charged with disposing of the government's vast surplus of war equipment and supplies.

Like Ike in Army vs. Jim Thorpe and Carlisle, Allen also had been involved in one of the most talked-about games in early college football history. His role, however, had not been that of a player, but as a quasi-athletic director.

In the early 1900s, Cumberland College had been a power in Southern football. The school dropped football in 1906 and resumed again in 1912. In 1916, Allen's involvement with the school's athletic program became noteworthy and may have also predicted his shortcomings as a lawyer as it highlighted his lack of attention to detail.

Allen had been student-manager of the 1915 baseball team. In 1916, the student-manager of the football team decided not to return to school and Allen assumed his duties. Shortly after taking over, Allen was told by Cumberland's president that the school was dropping football again because of a budget crunch. Allen was given the responsibility of contacting all the schools on the Cumberland schedule and canceling the games. Allen contacted all the schools but one. He overlooked Cumberland's game in Atlanta against Georgia Tech. When the omission was discovered, the scheduled date was almost at hand. Cumberland tried to back out of the game, but Tech was upset about losing a home date on such short notice and began rattling sabers about a cash forfeiture from Cumberland for failure to fulfill their contractual agreement.

What happened next gets pretty murky; Allen put together a team to play the game. There have been reports some members of the team were not actually students at Cumberland and that Allen received part of Cumberland's share of the gate receipts for his efforts. The game turned out to be one of the most famous contests in collegiate history, as Tech scored on every one of its offensive possessions and set a record for points scored that should stand forever, winning 222-0.

The Sunday before Ike departed for his 1955 after-the-Masters vacation at Augusta, Carey Middlecoff won the tournament by a seven-stroke margin. While Middlecoff was slipping into his green jacket, Ike was in Gettysburg, looking over the final decorative finishing touches Mamie had made on the interior of the house at the farm. The next day Ike and Mamie hosted the annual Easter Egg Roll on the White House Lawn. That afternoon, Ike handled his Opening Day first pitch duties and watched the Senators down the Baltimore Orioles. The next morning, he and Mamie departed for a nine-day vacation at Augusta National. Most of the gang was there for at least part of his stay. It was their first gathering since the announcement, six weeks earlier, that Bob Woodruff had offered the presidency of Coca-Cola to fellow gang member Bill Robinson and Robinson, who had earlier left the *New York Herald Tribune* to work for one of the country's top ad agencies, had accepted the post.

After his Augusta vacation, Ike spent almost every weekend in Gettysburg, checking on the progress of its finishing touches. On one of these trips, Ike flew up. Not in the six-engine Columbine III but in a small twin-engine Aero Commander he had begun using for short hops. On these Gettysburg weekends, Ike also got in some golf at what would become a regular venue for him—the Gettysburg Country Club. It was on the west side of town, just up the road from where Union cavalry had encountered a column of Confederate infantry and the first shots of the Battle of Gettysburg were fired. By no means was it on the level of the courses Ike typically played, but Ike seemed just as anxious to get to its first tee as he did Augusta National's. Then, as it is today, it is a nine-hole course that features two sets of tees for those who desire to play 18 holes, which Ike almost always did.

Over the July Fourth holiday period and as part of their 39th wedding anniversary celebration, Mamie and Ike held a party at the farm for over 150 members of the White House staff. Actually, it was two parties: an early session for staffers who had to work the evening shift and a later session for those who were off or who had worked the first shift at the White House.

The following week, Cliff Roberts, Ellis Slater, and a third member of Augusta National, Freeman Gosden, came to Washington on a sweltering day for a round with Ike at Burning Tree and a stag dinner at the White House that evening. Due to his work schedule, Gosden was a part-time member of the gang. After toiling for years on the Vaudeville circuit, he and his partner Charles Correll had hit it big in the 1930s when they created the *Amos and Andy* radio show, the story of two black men from Georgia who moved to Chicago to operate the Fresh Air Taxi Cab Company. Gosden played Amos, a hard-working church-goer who played life straight and believed in the basic goodness of his fellow man. Correll's character, Andy, was a deep-voiced, roly-poly, and gullible character. Gosden also did the voices for other characters in the show, such as the conniving George "Kingfish" Stevens and the slow-witted Lightnin'. The show was a phenomenal success. In order not to lose patrons, bars and restaurants made sure they had their radios on at seven every evening, and some movie houses would stop their features in mid-reel and bring a radio out on stage. In September 1948, Gosden and Correll would sell the rights to the show to CBS for a reported 2.5 million dollars, where it stayed in production until 1960. In the early 1950s, Correll and Gosden also produced the television version of the show that featured black actors in their parts.

Whereas Freeman Gosden's schedule kept him from the course, fellow gang member Bob Woodruff frequently chose not to play. When the gang was in Washington, he would regularly forego golf and join the group later at the White House for dinner and drinks. Often, Ann Whitman would arrange for the Coca-Cola magnate to be let in the back entrance.

Unlike Cliff Roberts and Pete Jones, Woodruff had been born into wealth but he was very much his own man. He was the gang member referenced in the Introduction that was said to have been born with a golden spoon in his mouth. It is also said his father immediately confiscated the spoon and melted it down for the bullion. His father was Ernest Woodruff an enormously successful Atlanta banker, who was as tight as they come and raised his children in a very penny-pinching environment.

Bob and his tight-fisted dad were never on the same page. Once Bob entered the business world after dropping out of college, his father tried to influence the career path he was taking. Bob would have none of it and cut ties with his father and struck out on his own. He became a very successful salesman with the White Motor Company and was soon sales manager of the southeast region.

In 1919, Ernest Woodruff had put together a syndicate and took over the Coca-Cola Company in what would be called today a leveraged buyout. Four years later, Coca-Cola needed fresh leadership at the top. His father offered the Coke presidency to Bob. The younger Woodruff had several other coals in the fire he was considering and there was considerable haggling back and forth concerning compensation. The son finally agreed to terms when he was assured he would be given free rein, which meant no interference from his old man. Bob Woodruff would guide the soft drink giant for the next 60 years and make Coke the world's most famous product.

Although he held memberships at the nation's golf Meccas —Augusta National, Burning Tree, and Cypress Point—Bob Woodruff was a poor golfer. He played the game for its business and political return. He did, however, like to wager on the course and was an aggressive negotiator for strokes. It is said that he would demand so many strokes that his good friend, Bobby Jones, couldn't even beat him.

Woodruff and Ike both excelled at annoying one another. Once during one of his evening trips to the White House, Woodruff and Ike became hopelessly at odds over an issue. Ike stated that he was retiring, and Woodruff followed him into the bedroom, still trying to make his case. Ike undressed, climbed into bed, and pulled the covers over his head until Woodruff departed. On another occasion, Ike was on a trip abroad and was photographed drinking a Coke through a straw. Woodruff angrily fired off a message to Ike requesting that in the future he not drink Coke from a straw in public. He was afraid Ike was giving the world the impression that Coke bottles were unsanitary.

There were certainly more cordial moments in their friendship. Once, when Ike called Woodruff at his Georgia plantation, the Coke czar had his vocally talented domestic staff serenade him over the phone with one of his favorite melodies.

Later in the summer of '55, almost everything seemed right with Ike's administration. The economy was booming, with more people working than ever before, and he had just concluded a summit meeting in Geneva, Switzerland, with Soviet Premier Nickolai Bulganin that had gone very well. "I Like Ike Fever" was at epidemic levels with a recent Gallup poll giving him an approval rating of 79 percent.

These high poll numbers could not be fully enjoyed by Republican Party leaders because Ike had not yet committed to run for a second term. And if he didn't, they were of the opinion there was not another Republican candidate who could win the presidency in the 1956 Election.

By the same token, the Democrats believed if Ike ran again, they would surely lose. With his high approval ratings and the overall strong condition of the country, they were desperate to find issues they could use against Ike. This desperation hit its peak at that year's United Auto Workers Convention, when Matthew Neely, a Democratic senator from West Virginia, addressing the gathering, questioned Ike's motives for attending church and highlighted the fact he had joined the Presbyterian Church only a few weeks after his inauguration in 1953. The senator's comments brought a torrid response from clergy, church-goers from all denominations, and editorial pages. Within 48 hours, Neely backed off his comments, stating his remarks had been misunderstood because of the way they had been reported. He was in fact criticizing the press for coverings Ike's church attendance.

There were signs retirement was weighing heavily on Ike's mind. For example, at a meeting with Republican leaders, he cautioned them not to attach all their hopes to the mast of one ship. Also, there was an indication Ike was concerned with his own mortality. During a recent stay at Gettysburg, he had sent his Aero Commander to Charlotte, N.C., to pick up a fellow avid golfer, the Reverend Billy Graham, and bring him to the farm in Gettysburg on a Sunday afternoon to discuss the hereafter.

A few days later at Andrews Air Force Base, Ike boarded his plane for what was scheduled to be a six-week vacation in Denver. But once Ike was on board, members of the press corps, used to quick takeoffs, wondered why the plane did not begin to taxi. In a few minutes they had their answer as they heard Ike's pilot exclaim, "Here comes Moaney now." They looked out and saw the President's valet scurrying for the plane with his boss' golf clubs.

6

THE BIG ONE

By this time, the Augusta National gang's annual journey to play golf with Ike in Denver had become so involved it was given a code name as if it were a military exercise: Operation Rocky Mountains. Cliff Roberts was the self-appointed supreme commander of the operation and he executed the gang's assault on Denver with the same precision and attention to detail he applied each year to his management of the Masters Golf Tournament.

The participants totaled 20. Roberts coordinated their arrival by corporate and commercial aircraft and then had them whisked away to Denver's famed Brown Derby Hotel in limousines provided by the Chrysler Corporation. Once at the Derby, the gang was treated to fine food and drink and the next morning they rendezvoused with Ike at Cherry Hills to begin three days of golf in a number of competitive formats. It was a particularly good gathering for Ellis Slater who, during one of the rounds, scored a hole-in-one at the par-three 15th hole.

At the conclusion of the weekend, Ike asked Slater and Pete Jones to return to Denver the following weekend for a stag dinner, which they did. At this gathering, Ike took Slater and Jones aside and told them he was upset by the number of members of his administration who were expressing the opinion that it was a foregone conclusion he would seek a second term.

During this Denver hiatus, Ike's routine mirrored that of the previous two years; in the morning he was at his office at Lowery and in the afternoon he played golf. At the office on this trip, he had some golf-related matters to attend to. He had to apply some pressure to the Membership Committee at Burning Tree. They had originally turned down the application by the Japanese ambassador for membership but after a little jawboning on Ike's part, the Burning Tree president soon sent word back to the Summer White House that the committee had reconsidered and the ambassador was going to be accepted into the membership. Additionally, since Ike was not going to personally be able to attend, he sent a congratulatory statement that was going to be read at a dinner in Atlanta in late September, honoring Bobby Jones on the 25th anniversary of his winning golf's Grand Slam. It read:

No one would be more delighted than I if, at this moment, I could be in Atlanta joined with his other friends in tribute to Bob Jones on the Twenty-fifth Anniversary of his Grand Slam.

That victory won him fame. But Bob Jones himself—the

man, the good citizen and good neighbor—by his life and great human qualities has won the enduring affection of the Nation.

As a golfer, the standards he sets in play and sportsmanship challenge the will of all who would excel in any pursuit. As a citizen of courage, stout heart, unfaltering optimism and abiding faith, he is an inspiration to all his countrymen.

Although I cannot be seated at the table with you, I am there in spirit—honoring my good friend, Bob Jones.

Sincerely,

Dwight D. Eisenhower

Also while he was at his Lowery Office, Ike received the Annual Report of Augusta National. In the financial section, it was reported the Masters Tournament provided a net profit to the club of $3,664 compared to a net profit of $8,805 from the previous year and that yearly dues were being raised from $350.00 to $400.00.

As his Denver stay was winding down, Ike left Denver and went back to Aksel Nielsen's place in the Rockies for five days of fishing and painting. Nielsen had recently upgraded the property with a prefabricated cabin that had an up-to-date kitchen for Ike to cook. For Ike's fishing pleasure, Nielsen had built a pond, and the week before Ike arrived, had it stocked with 400 rainbow trout. Accompanying Ike were George Allen, who had been in Denver for several weeks, and Assistant Press Secretary Murray Snyder.

While there, Ike fished to his heart's content, dabbled with some painting, and hit a few golf balls at a target his Secret

Service detail had set up. He also did all the cooking for the party. On his last morning there, Ike was out of bed at 5 a.m. He cooked the party a hearty breakfast of fried eggs with bacon and sausage. At 6:45, he departed for Denver. His motorcade made the 70-mile trip in an hour and forty minutes. He stopped by his mother-in-law's home to freshen up and was in his office at Lowery by 9 a.m. While there, he spent much of the time on the phone in conversation with Washington, reviewed a letter from Soviet Premier Nikolai Bulganin, and sent get-well wishes to the Democrats' leader in the Senate, Lyndon Johnson, who was at his Texas ranch recovering from a recent heart attack.

Ike then headed out to Cherry Hills. After about a 20-minute warm-up session, he teed off with George Allen and Cherry Hills golf professional Rip Arnold. Following along with the trio was a 74-year-old man named Howard Snyder, Ike's physician.

Nicknamed "Old Duck" by Ann Whitman, Snyder had been Mamie's doctor during the war and became Ike's physician when he returned from Europe. When Ike became president, Snyder was named his White House physician.

Not everyone thought Dr. Snyder was up to the job of being the President of the United States' physician. He had been out of medical school for almost 50 years when he was given the task of caring for the most powerful person in the world, and many of his peers felt he had not kept abreast of the advances in medicine.

Former aides have stated Snyder's presence would often make Ike nervous and irritable because Snyder was constantly trying to take his blood pressure and administer shots in his posterior. Ike contended these shots were more painful than they should have been because Snyder had a slight tremor in his shot hand.

That afternoon at Cherry Hills, Ike was really enjoying his round until word came there was a message from Washington. State-of-the-art presidential communication at that time required Ike to go back to the clubhouse to use a secure land-line. When Ike reached the clubhouse, he became very irritated as he was told Secretary of State John Foster Dulles had wanted to talk with him but he had ended the call because he had to go to a meeting and would call back in an hour.

An hour later, Ike put his round on hold and returned to the clubhouse, only to be told there was a problem with the phone lines and that he would be notified as soon as the difficulty was corrected. Ike had just resumed play when he was informed the call from Dulles had come through, and he dashed back to the clubhouse to take it. After concluding the call, Ike completed his round, shooting an 84. He then had lunch at the clubhouse, a hamburger steak smothered in onions. After lunch, Ike decided since his round had been interrupted so many times, he wanted to play nine more holes.

Shortly after starting the third nine, Ike was called off the course for the fourth time to take another call from Dulles. When he got to the clubhouse, he was told there had been a miscommunication; Dulles was not trying to reach him again. Ike was beyond furious. According to Dr. Snyder, the veins on Ike's forehead were bulging so much they looked like cords on a whip. Later, on his 26th hole of the day, Ike complained about chest pain and remarked that he thought the onions he had eaten with lunch were backing up on him. The pain appeared to be a passing thing. He went on to play out that hole and the last one, posting a score for that nine of 42. Later, in the locker room, Ike appeared to be his bouncy self again, chatting with Rip Arnold while changing from his golf clothes and recalling that Cherry Hills Country Club had been where he had played his first round of golf 30 years before.

After departing Cherry Hills, Ike returned to his mother-in law's home, where he painted for a couple of hours. The George Allens came over for dinner but Ike displayed little appetite during the meal. After a short period of socializing, the Allens departed, and Ike retired at about 10:00 p.m.

As was almost always the case when Ike was away from Washington, Ann Whitman was part of the support team that accompanied him. At 6:45 a.m. the next morning (Saturday), Ann was awakened in her Denver quarters by a phone call. On the other end of the line was Dr. Snyder. He advised her that Ike would not be in early to his office that morning but that he might show up at around 10:00 a.m. He then instructed her to tell Assistant Press Secretary Murray Snyder (Jim Hagerty was taking some time off back in Washington) if the press asked any questions to tell them the president was suffering from a digestive upset. Since Ike had a history of stomach problems, Whitman passed on the message to Murray Snyder without a second thought.

Almost four hours earlier, Dr. Snyder had also been awakened in his Denver quarters by a phone call. On the line was Mamie Eisenhower, and there was an alarming tone in her voice. She told Snyder to come quickly. Ike was having chest pain. Snyder called for a car and driver, threw a coat over his pajamas, and raced out the door.

Thirty minutes before, Mamie had been returning from the bathroom and heard Ike tossing about in his bed. She went to his bedside and asked him if he was having a nightmare. Ike told her no and thanked her for checking. She then returned to her bedroom. Twenty minutes later, Ike came to her bedside, complaining of lower chest pain, and asked her to give him a dose of Milk of Magnesia. When Mamie turned the light on, she was alarmed by Ike's skin color. She found the Milk of Magnesia and gave him a dose. She then placed the called to Dr. Snyder.

According to handwritten notes he indicated were made at Ike's bedside several hours after his arrival and just after he had placed the call to Ann Whitman, Snyder wrote that as soon as he arrived and listened to Ike's heart and took his blood pressure; he knew it was "a heart injury." He then gave Ike three injections: one to dilate his arteries, one to prevent blood clotting, and morphine to reduce his pain. Snyder attempted to administer oxygen from the tank he brought with him but Ike was too agitated and would not tolerate the mask. When Ike asked for more relief from his pain, Snyder injected him with another dose of morphine. Mamie had earlier awakened Sergeant Moaney to help her attend to Ike. Snyder instructed Moaney to rub Ike down with alcohol while he and Mamie placed hot water bottles around his body. Ike's skin began to show signs of cool perspiration, and he went into a state of shock.

For the next 20 minutes, Ike's condition wavered. Snyder

made no attempt to summon additional assistance. Hoping to calm Ike down and warm his body, he instructed Mamie to get into bed with Ike and nuzzle her body against his. Almost immediately, Ike became calm and fell asleep.

At 8:00 a.m. Saturday morning, the press corps was told the President of the United States had an upset stomach, and that story immediately went out to media outlets across the country. A couple of hours later, members of the press were asking Ann Whitman to call Dr. Snyder to get a confirmation on whether the president's condition was or was not serious. Whitman sent a message to Doctor Snyder, and in 45 minutes, he sent word back that the president's "digestive upset" was not serious. At noon, Murray Snyder passed on Dr. Snyder's most recent message on Ike's condition to the press corps and recommended it might be a good weekend for them to take some time off.

At about this same time, which was nine hours after he first examined Ike, Dr. Snyder called the commanding general at nearby Fitzsimmons Army Hospital and asked him to send a cardiologist to the summer White House. The Fitzsimmons' doctor was there in short order and ran an EKG on Ike. The EKG revealed Ike had suffered a heart attack.

It was decided to take Ike to Fitzsimmons by car instead of by ambulance. His Secret Service driver and Sergeant Moaney walked Ike down the stairs and out to the car. The driver was instructed to take a circuitous route to the hospital to make sure they were not being followed by the press. Ike was allowed to sit up on the trip to the hospital. He was in a haze as a result of the morphine and repeatedly asked about the whereabouts of his wallet. When they reached Fitzsimmons, Ike was quickly whisked away in a wheelchair to the hospital's VIP suite on its eighth floor.

Once Ike was in the hospital, Murray Snyder was informed of what had really happened, and he called Jim Hagerty in Washington. Hagerty had just gotten home from playing in a golf tournament at Columbia Country Club. He was reading the afternoon paper, which was reporting that Ike experienced stomach problems during the night, when he got the call. He and Murray Snyder went over what was going to be said in the official announcement of the heart attack, which Snyder was going to make at a press conference 30 minutes after the call. Hagerty used the 30 minutes to contact Vice-President Nixon and cabinet members to forewarn them of the impending announcement.

In a few hours, Hagerty and Dr. Thomas Mattingly, Ike's cardiologist at Walter Reed Army Hospital, were taking off for Denver on a military plane. Also on the flight was Merriman Smith of United Press International, the longtime dean of the White House corps, who after enduring Ike's two previous long summer vacations in Denver had decided to take a break and stay home in Washington. After hearing the news about Ike that afternoon, he had contacted Hagerty and begged his way onto the flight.

When Ike took the oath of office for his first term, Smith, who would later win a Pulitzer Prize in 1964 for his coverage of the Kennedy assassination, was near the halfway point of his three-decade run on the White House beat. Known for his competitiveness and aggressiveness, Smith once fell and broke his shoulder while running for a phone to call in his story after an important FDR news conference. He sprang back up, found a phone, called in his report, and then headed for the hospital.

Smith, another frequent player at President Truman's poker table, was fascinated by everything a Commander-in-Chief did and anything that happened at the White House. He was in tight with the Secret Service and with the administrative and support personnel. He was obviously very tight with Ann Whitman. She wrote to a friend prior to leaving for this trip to Denver, "I sadly predict a quite boring time out there [Denver] because my special friends Tom Stephens [Ike's appointment secretary] and Merriman Smith aren't going to be there."

According to Dr. Mattingly, during the flight Smith sat down beside him and abruptly asked him why Ike's previous heart attacks had never been reported to the public. Mattingly was taken aback by Smith's question. Smith pushed the matter, getting right in Mattingly's face pressing for an answer. At that point, Mattingly broke off the exchange, stating he needed to get some rest, and went to the rear of the plane. Hagerty was a silent witness to the exchange. Once he was situated in the rear of the plane, Mattingly didn't rest; he was carrying Ike's medical records and history. Perplexed by Smith's accusations, he reviewed them, looking for any sign or evidence of prior heart trouble. He found none.

Ann Whitman had spent most of that afternoon trying to get in touch with the members of the gang. She reached Cliff Roberts, who was in New York City, shortly after he had returned from an afternoon round at Blind Brook Country Club. When Ann told him what had happened, Roberts told her a civilian physician needed be brought in to assist in Ike's care. After hanging up with Whitman, he called Vice President Nixon, Secretary of the Treasury George Humphrey, and Jerry Persons, a retired general who was now one of Ike's top aides, and told them the same thing. Within a few hours of those conversations, it was announced that Paul Dudley White, a world-renowned cardiologist from Boston, had boarded a military plane and was being flown to Denver to head up Ike's medical team.

Early the next morning, Dr. Snyder sought out Mattingly. Snyder was beside himself over the firestorm of criticism he was receiving in the press over his handling of Ike's attack: his initial report that it was a digestive upset, not having him brought directly to the hospital, not calling for additional assistance for almost nine hours, not using an ambulance for transport, and allowing Ike to walk out to the car. Actually, Mattingly was asking himself the same questions, but in deference to Snyder's agitated state, he told him things would probably die down in a day or so and for him not to worry. Dr. White arrived several hours later, and he and Mattingly went together to the hospital to see Ike for the first time.

White spent about 15 minutes examining and chatting with Ike. He was satisfied with the treatment Ike was receiving. He then met with Mamie Eisenhower. Later, he met with Vice President Nixon, who had just arrived on the scene, and Jim Hagerty.

White and Mattingly were given quarters at the Officers Club, which was a short distance from the hospital. Across the street from their quarters was a golf course. Appropriately enough, that evening, the two doctors took a walk around the course to discuss Ike's care and the press conference that was going to be held the next day. Both doctors believed Ike's treatment was going satisfactorily. As for the press conference, White conceived the plan that the best thing to do would be to give the press and the nation a course in myocardial infarction. Mattingly also brought up his conversation with Merriman Smith. White shared Mattingly's opinion that Ike's records did not show any indication of a prior heart attack.

If ever there had been the right man at the right place at the right time, it was Dr. White. He had been one of the principals in the founding of the American Heart Association and was well known and well regarded in the national media. As he had treated William Randolph Hearst, Albert Schweitzer, and Cornelius Vanderbilt, Dr. White had plenty of experience with high-profile patients. He also possessed a perfect bedside manner, which he had for years adeptly applied to his individual patients and their families. White was a man who inspired confidence, which was suddenly in short supply in the nation. When he began treating the nation at the press conference on Monday at 10:00 a.m. Mountain Time, on its first trading day since Ike's attack, Wall Street was reflecting the panic-stricken mood of the country, with stock prices having their worst day since the crash of 1929.

White's opening remarks at the news conference quickly had the press corps in the palm of his hand. "The coronary muscle as you know, are small arteries that supply the heart muscle with blood. And this is fundamentally, you see, an arterial disease and not primarily a heart disease. It is the arteries that are affected. But they are the arteries that supply the heart muscle with blood, so they involve the heart secondarily."

The press was taking notes as if a college professor were telling his students what questions were going to be on the final exam. White went on to cover the number of coronary arteries, their sizes, and the number of branches each had. From there, he moved on to other factors, such as family history, age, diet, and personal habits and lifestyle, and how the thickening of the arterial wall affected the bore of the artery.

White also brought up the point some people were speculating about: that the 27 holes of golf Ike had played the day before might have been instrumental in bringing on the attack. White stated he believed it had no bearing on the attack.

Merriman Smith was present at the press conference but he did not broach the prior heart attack issue. And to Dr. White and Mattingly's surprise, there were no questions from the press about Snyder's handling of events prior to Ike's arrival at the hospital.

Over the next several days and weeks in correspondence with Ike's brothers and his own medical and army friends, Dr. Snyder offered the following as his reasons for not calling for additional assistance, delaying Ike's transport to the hospital, and the digestive upset story:

It was difficult for me to assume the responsibility of refraining from making publicly immediately the diagnosis of coronary thrombosis. I postponed public announcement because I wished the president to benefit from the rest and quiet induced

by the sedation incident to combating the initial manifesta-
tions. This decision also spared him, his wife, and mother-in-
law emotional upset attendant upon to precipitate announcement of serious import. The end result was that all who were
intimately concerned were much better able to accept the information, delivered by suggestion during the intermediate hours
of rest which were afforded the President. This action, I believe,
limited the heart damage to a minimum and enabled us to
make an unhurried transference from home to hospital.

While the nation prayed for Ike's recovery, it was a foregone
conclusion by the press and the public that Ike's heart attack
would take him out of the political arena. The Republicans
were taking a standing eight count with respect to their holding
onto the White House in 1956, while Democrats were experi-
encing a political resurrection from what appeared to be a lost
cause to almost a sure win in the next election.

Back at Fitzsimmons Army Hospital, the eighth floor
became the forerunner of today's coronary care units, with
shifts of cardiologists, specialized nurses, technicians, and
other support personnel on duty around the clock. After a brief
setback, Ike began his journey down the road to recovery.

Within six weeks after the attack, doctors felt Ike was ready
to be released from Fitzsimmons. Ike balked, however, at being
released when he was told he would have to board his plane for
Washington in a wheelchair. He opted to stay in the hospital
another week so he would be strong enough to walk up the
steps onto the plane. To make sure he could do it, he spent the
next week practicing, walking up a 14-step stairwell.

On November 11, 51 days after the attack, Ike walked briskly up the steps of the Columbine III's ramp and gave a big wave and a big grin to the crowd. When he arrived at the airport in Washington, a crowd of 5000 was there to welcome him and tremendous crowds lined the path of his motorcade to the White House. On Constitution Avenue the procession passed under a large banner mounted above the street. It read: "WELCOME HOME, IKE."

Ike stayed in Washington for a few days and then went to his Gettysburg farm for an extended period of recuperation. The Professional Golfers Association stepped in to aid in his recovery by having a practice putting green installed just a few paces from his side porch at Gettysburg.

Many believed that, up until this time, Ike had given up on thoughts of a second term. Those who had contact with him at Gettysburg during this period indicated he appeared to be depressed. He would spend long periods just sitting in a chair. When he did move about the house, he used a putter as a cane. But letters of encouragement from old friends and total strangers who had suffered heart attacks soon apparently began to change Ike's attitude.

Ike's recovery outlook was also being buoyed by a member of the opposition party, the man he had sent speedy recovery wishes to from his heart attack just hours before he suffered his own—Lyndon Johnson. LBJ was running people over on the comeback trail and he would soon be returning to a leadership position in the Senate and in his party.

It certainly was not good news, however, when Ike learned while he was convalescing at Gettysburg that Cliff Roberts had suffered a heart attack. Roberts, who had been the first nonfamily member allowed to visit Ike in Denver after his heart attack, had left his Manhattan hotel on a brisk January evening for a walk. During the walk, he began to experience some tightness in his chest and shortness of breath. Roberts returned to his hotel and shortly thereafter he began feeling woozy. He called for the hotel doctor and was soon being transported to the hospital. At the hospital, doctors concluded he had suffered a "mild heart attack." Although his heart attack was certainly not as severe as Ike's, Roberts' recovery proved to be another positive example for him, because his close friend was practically back to his normal daily life in just 30 days.

As Ike's spirits and health began to improve, his feelings about seeking reelection shifted dramatically toward another run. This notion was also supported by Mamie. She had originally wanted him to step aside in 1956. But after seeing how unhappy he was during the initial phase of his recovery period, she was now of the opinion he was not ready for retirement.

With each passing day, Ike's personal and political future began looking stronger and stronger. The political outlook was being masterfully handled by the excellent work with the press by Jim Hagerty. As far as Ike was concerned, Hagerty had started off his spin on his chief's recovery process with a tee shot that went way out of bounds when, during a press conference describing Ike's condition, Hagerty stunned the press corps and much of the world by reporting Ike had had a good bowel movement that morning. But from that point on, Ike would have been hard-pressed to question any part of Hagerty's handling of the press as he soon had them and the rest of the country thinking very positively about Ike's future.

The first week in January, Ike went to Key West for a week. He was joined by most of the members of the gang, and they played a lot of bridge. Ike also began to work on his short game, practicing pitch shots daily at a baseball field. He held a press conference on the last day of the trip and many in the press corps remarked he had never looked or sounded better. Shortly after returning to Washington, Ike held a meeting with his most-trusted advisors on whether he should seek a second term. The consensus was that he should. There was one major hurdle, however, which had to be cleared before the final decision could be made. It was the report on his physical condition in mid-February by his medical team.

Dr. Paul Dudley White, as head of the team, would render the report. His involvement in the treatment of Ike after the attack had boosted his reputation even higher, but he was looked upon by his famous patient as a bit of a loose cannon. Publicly, White was indicating that Ike was in the condition to seek a second term, but privately he was trying to dissuade him. Although he thought it would be good for Ike to keep working, he favored a less-demanding position like "Goodwill Ambassador for World Peace."

Ike did some behind-the-scenes maneuvering to get White on the right course. The press conference during which White was to issue the final report was still a matter of much concern because not only would what White have tremendous weight, but also the way he said it would be equally important. White's performance when issuing the report was the same high-caliber and confidence-building type as his first news conference after Ike's attack. He cleared the way for Ike to seek a second term with the following statement:

Now as to the future, after weighing carefully all available evidence, including our own experience, and fully aware of the hazards and uncertainties that lie ahead, we believe that medically the chances are that the President should be able to carry on an active life satisfactorily for another five to 10 years.

Ike's medical team was also quizzed at the press conference about when he would return to the golf course. The consensus was he would gradually begin to play a few holes at a time. In approximately six weeks, they expected he would be capable of playing a full 18 holes.

After the medical team's report, Ike left for a vacation at the plantation of his Secretary of Labor, George Humphrey, near Thomasville, Georgia. Two days after arriving, he showed up at the Glen Arven Country Club in Thomasville and played his first golf since his heart attack. He played nine holes in a steady drizzle with Jim Hagerty, the club pro, and the club president. As he stepped onto the first tee, he told the large crowd of reporters and photographers, "I have been waiting for this for a long time."

During his rehab, Ike was only allowed to practice three-quarter swings and this was going to be the first time he had been permitted to make a full swing. He admitted to feeling tentative on his swings, and it showed. Ike took the liberty of hitting three shots off the first tee. Taking the best of the three, he went on to shoot a 47 for the nine holes.

A photo of Ike on the first tee was on the front page of almost every paper in the country the next day. Five days later, what the *New York Times* called "the most politically significant round of golf ever played" took place in Thomasville. Ike returned to Glenn Arven to play what was scheduled to be another nine-hole round. To everyone's surprise, Ike kept going at the turn and played a full 18 holes. To all the press corps, he looked and acted like the old Ike. He could be heard setting the wagers on the first tee and giving his opponents some needling.

Spectators and the press were allowed only to observe the first and the last hole on each side. On the 18th hole, a par three, Ike hit a poor tee shot and still had a wedge to the green for his second shot. The crowd at the green cheered when Ike pitched his ball to within a few feet of the hole. Unfortunately for Ike, his putting was rusty and when he missed the short putt for his par the crowd groaned like he had just lost the U.S. Open.

Dr. Snyder was quizzed by reporters after the round whether Ike was not pushing it a bit by playing 18 holes four weeks sooner than had been expected. Snyder replied, "All he needs is a good game—that will keep him healthy and well." He then pointed to Ike's pitch shot at the last hole and said, "That will keep him happy for a long time."

Several days after returning to Washington, Ike made it official and announced he would run again.

7

ON THE OPERATING TABLE

During Ike's recovery period, the White House mail room had been swamped with "get well" wishes and letters in which the writer had overcome serious health issues, diet tips, and, of course, an abundance of golf tips.

One of the golf tip letters reached Ike during his stay in Thomasville. It was from a Chicago executive who had developed his own in-office practice set-up. He claimed it had done wonders for his game and he had included detailed instructions on what Ike would need to implement the program in the Oval Office. Ike was intrigued by the set-up and wrote back to the man, thanking him for the information and stating he planned to study his material in more detail when he returned to Washington.

Part of the Chicago executive's instructions for his in-office practice regimen was that Ike's staff would have to keep him from being disturbed for two fifteen-minute periods during the day. This would not have been a problem for Ike because he had the ultimate gatekeeper in Sherman Adams, his chief of staff.

Adams was a former governor of New Hampshire. He had been instrumental in Ike's primary victory there in his battle against Taft for the Republican nomination in 1952. When he became Ike's top aide, he quickly earned a reputation for rudeness and ruthlessness, but he was evenhanded; he rubbed as many Republicans the wrong way as he did Democrats. Those who worked with him believed he had created the word *no* and had never been informed about the use of *good-bye* as after he was finished talking with someone over the phone, he would just hang up.

The only person Adams seemed not to rub the wrong way was Ike. He knew Adams had a tough job and liked the way he carried it out, and Adams had deep respect for his boss. He played golf with Ike only a couple of times during his tenure, but he was a regular at the afternoon practice sessions on the South Lawn. He would go over government appointments, pending legislation, and other matters with Ike while he worked on his eight-iron shots.

Ike's golf game would often add to Adams' work load. Such was the case while Ike was playing golf in Thomasville; Adams was handling a golf-related problem back at the White House. For the second time in four years, Ike's annual week after the Masters trip to Augusta National had collided with the Washington Senators' American League opener.

This would be Ike's first trip to Augusta since his heart attack and there was no way he was going to adjust his schedule, so Adams stepped up to the plate to resolve the problem. He worked with Senators' owner Clark Griffith and the American League office to reschedule the game so they would have Ike present. The rescheduled date had to be rescheduled, but Adams finally got the American League's season opener on a date that did not conflict with Ike's golf at Augusta. It turned out to be a good game, if you were a New York Yankees' fan. The defending American League Champions pounded the Senators 10-4. Ike stayed for the entire contest, which featured two tape-measure home run blasts by Yankee superstar Mickey Mantle.

As the calendar rolled into June of 1956, Ike was getting in plenty of golf at Burning Tree and looking stronger and stronger. But things were about to change dramatically. Ike would find himself in the deep rough again both physically and politically—all because of a little roughage.

On the evening of June 7th, Ike attended the White House Photographers Association Dinner at Washington's Sheraton-Park Hotel which featured entertainment by Bob Hope and rhythm-and-blues songstress Pearl Bailey.

Ike's doctor would have been proud at his selections off the menu. For his soup, he passed on the thick soup on the bill of fare and requested a cup of clear consommé. For his main course, he had a small filet mignon with green beans instead of a baked potato. If only he had been that selective at a luncheon at the White House earlier that day.

Since his early Army days, Ike had been beset with stomach problems and for some time Dr. Snyder had directed him not to eat raw vegetables. But at lunch he asked Charles, his butler at the White House, to bring him a Waldorf salad. Charles knew of the doctor's orders on no raw vegetables, but elected not to challenge the President of the United States on his dietary restrictions.

Ike returned to the White House from the dinner at the Park-Sheraton at 11:00 p.m. In what was very close to a replay of those early morning hours almost eight months before in Denver, Mamie was on the phone to Dr. Snyder at 12:45 a.m. She told him Ike was tossing and turning in his bed with a stomach ache. Snyder told her to give a small dose of Milk of Magnesia, then he bid Mamie good-night and rolled over in his bed and went back to sleep.

Thirty-five minutes later, Mamie called Snyder and asked him to please come to the White House. Snyder's Connecticut Avenue apartment was only a mile away and he was there in a matter of minutes. He spent the night sitting by Ike's bed. He gave Ike some tea with sugar at about 7:00 a.m. but Ike couldn't keep it down and then as the morning progressed, Ike vomited several more times.

It became apparent to Snyder this wasn't Ike's run-of-the-mill belly ache. He called for the Chief of Medicine at Walter Reed to come to the White House and sent out calls to have Dr. Paul Dudley White and Dr. Thomas Mattingly respond as well. White was on a plane from Boston in short order. Mattingly was a little tougher to reach; he was headed south on vacation. Snyder put the Secret Service on the case. In short order, Mattingly was pulled over by the South Carolina Highway Patrol. Sixty minutes later, he was strapped into a T-33 Jet trainer that was roaring at full throttle toward Washington.

At 1:00 p.m. in the afternoon, Ike was transported from the

White House in an Army ambulance to Walter Reed. An electrocardiogram, along with other tests, showed his heart was sound; an X-ray revealed an obstruction in the small intestine. It was suspected this intestinal obstruction was due to ileitis (inflammation of the lower portion of the small intestine).

It was the consensus among the surgeons and specialists now involved with Ike's stomach problem that they should take the conservative approach and see if the obstruction would pass by ordinary means. Over the next 10 hours, however, Ike's condition only worsened. At a midnight meeting of the doctors, it was decided they would have to do what none of them were anxious to do—operate on the President of the United States.

The operation began three hours later and lasted almost two hours. The obstruction was a small piece of celery from the Waldorf salad which had become lodged in the small intestine which had been constricted by an attack of ileitis.

Physically, Ike's doctors were confident he would have a full recovery. A full recovery politically was quite another matter. With the Republican Convention less than 60 days away, Ike would need to look the picture of health for voters as his party went through the formality of re-nominating him, because the Democrats and a number of members of the press were attempting to make his health a major issue.

Ike's doctors predicted his recovery from the surgery would take six weeks. In mid-July, just two days short of that time frame, Ike flew to Panama and withstood the rigors of a conference of Latin American leaders that lasted for five days.

On August 4th, albeit for just four holes, Ike went out to Burning Tree and played golf for the first time since his surgery.

On August 9th, he returned to Burning Tree and played nine holes. Two days before the start of the Democratic Convention in Chicago on August 11th, he was back out at Burning Tree for another nine.

At their convention in Chicago, the Democrats re-nominated Adlai Stevenson and placed Tennessee Senator Estes Kefauver on the ticket as his running mate.

Two weeks later, Ike flew to the Republican Convention in San Francisco to accept the party's presidential nomination. After his acceptance speech, he was driven down from San Francisco to Monterey, California, for four days of golf at Cypress Point with members of the gang, playing a full 18 holes each day. While Ike was enjoying golf at one of the game's top venues, the Democrats were getting into the mail 100,000 copies of their game plan for the election, *The Democratic National Committee 1956 Campaign Fact Book*. The 110-page manual was being sent to all state and county party leaders, candidates, and campaign committees.

The manual left no doubt Ike's health was going to be an issue in the campaign. One of its sections was: "Will President's Illness Curtail Vital Activities." It noted the following:

Medical authorities believe there is a 35 to 60 percent chance of recurrence in the ileitis, the abdominal ailment for which the President underwent surgery.

A standard insurance manual "Risk Appraisal" calls ileitis "always serious" and advises "positively no" as to disability insurance for ileitis sufferers.

Army medical regulations disqualify for a commission anyone who has suffered a coronary attack like the President's.

The book then added that the President, as Commander-in-Chief, obviously carries much greater burdens and responsibility than does the ordinary commissioned officer.

The manual also recommended that the Democrats hit hard on Ike's vacation habits and to use a *U.S. News and World Report* article that calculated Ike's average vacation time during his first term to be 81 days a year.

The day Ike arrived back in Washington from his golf at Cypress Point, Stevenson was on the attack out on the stump in Oregon, railing about Ike and using a golf analogy. "I hope my opponent has time to face some of the realities of our diminished stature in the world and lost opportunities at home and when I speak of 'lost opportunities,' I don't mean on the putting green."

In an editorial, *The New York Daily News* called Stevenson out for what it called "his prissy little jabs at Eisenhower's golf," noting there were 3,500,000 U.S. golfers and concluded, "In sneering at golf, a politician takes much the same risk as in sneering at Baseball, Baby, Mother, the Flag, the Home or the Dog."

Ike took a commanding lead in the polls from the outset of the campaign. And despite the golf criticism and questions about his health, his lead remained as solid as Ben Hogan's golf swing throughout the campaign.

In a desperate attempt to turn the tide in the closing days of the campaign, Stevenson zeroed in on Ike's heart attack. During a nationally televised speech, he stated, "Every piece of available medical evidence we have, and I hate to say it, suggests Vice President Richard Nixon will be President within four years if Eisenhower is re-elected President." The statement did not gain Stevenson any additional support. In fact, many believed it actually cost him votes. Ike was easily swept back into office, winning all but seven Southern states. So complete was the rout that Robert Kennedy, who had worked in Stevenson's campaign, later admitted he had actually voted for Ike.

One can only speculate how close this election would have been, or, if Ike would have even been the Republican Party nominee, if the future Pulitzer-Prize-winning journalist Merriman Smith had put into print his contention that the heart attack Ike suffered in Denver was not his first. Over 20 years after Ike left office and a dozen years after his death, another person joined Smith in the "previous heart attack" camp: the man he had confronted about the issue on their flight to Denver, Ike's cardiologist, Dr. Thomas Mattingly.

In 1967, seven years after he left office, Ike sent Dr. Mattingly a copy of his recently released memoir, *At Ease*. In the book, Ike described his 1949 illness. Although it had been reported in the press, Mattingly had missed it; neither was there any trace of the illness in Ike's medical history. During a subsequent examination of Ike, Mattingly tried to broach the subject of that illness with him but Ike would only say it was a collapse. The tone of Ike's response to his inquiry gave Mattingly the impression it was a touchy subject.

After striking out with Ike, Mattingly reached out to Dr. Snyder for information on the 1949 illness. By this time "Old Duck" was in his late 80s and had suffered a series of strokes. And as a result, Mattingly could glean no additional information on the subject from him and he dropped the matter.

Mattingly's interest was rekindled in 1982, 13 years after Ike's death and 12 years after Snyder had passed away, thanks to a chance meeting with Dr. Charles Leedham, a retired Army internist, at a conference of medical consultants to the Armed Forces. During a conversation between the two, Leedham, according to Mattingly, rather boastfully stated he had treated Ike for a heart attack while he was chief of medicine at the Army's Oliver General Hospital in Augusta. Leedham was unsure of the exact date, but claimed the treatment took place between 1947 and 1950. Leedham also stated Ike's treatment had been a hush-hush affair and only Dr. Snyder and Ike's aide, Colonel Charles Shultz, were present when he treated him.

After the conference, Mattingly made a number of attempts to obtain additional information by phone and letter from Dr. Leedham but in Mattingly's terms Leedham had "clammed up."

In spite of the absence of cooperation from Leedham, Mattingly chose to keep pursuing the matter. After much time and effort, he could produce no hard evidence but his investigation produced enough circumstantial evidence to lead him to believe Ike suffered a heart attack in 1949 and possibly another one in 1953.

To reach this conclusion, Mattingly made a review of all the medical records on Ike at the office of the Surgeon General of the Army. He was also given access to Snyder's personal papers and he did extensive research of the medical records available on Ike at the Eisenhower Library.

In the Surgeon General's records, Mattingly was able to verify at least one part of Leedham's story, as he found records of lab work performed on Ike at Oliver General Hospital in

Augusta in April 1949. He also found an EKG that was performed at Key West in 1949 he believed could be interpreted as revealing a heart attack.

What was absent from Ike's records was also revealing. Mattingly could not find any record of Ike being treated at Walter Reed Hospital in March of 1949. This lack of records conflicts with the memory of the man who had succeeded Ike as Chief of the Army 15 months earlier, Omar Bradley, who recalled that Ike was at Walter Reed before he left for Key West.

A heavy smoker since his West Point days, Ike quit cold turkey during the 1949 illness. Mattingly believed he did this because of his heart as well and this hypothesis was supported by a conversation Ike reportedly had with Clare Booth Luce, the wife of Henry Luce, the publisher of *Time* and *Life* magazines, and an accomplished playwright, journalist, and politician in her own right. The conversation took place sometime after the 1949 illness and in it, Ike was said to have told Mrs. Luce the reason he gave up smoking was "a little heart trouble."

Mattingly also found in Snyder's records a letter he had written to Mamie's family's physician in Denver, Dr. Herbert A. Black. It was dated the day after Snyder had brought Ike up from Key West to Augusta National. Due to the great lengths Snyder went to in his letter to discount the fact this illness was in any way heart-related, Mattingly became convinced it was "planted" as part of a paper trail designed to steer away any later scrutiny of this illness from the heart.

These items, coupled with Snyder's baffling decision not to call for additional assistance in Denver for almost nine hours after he responded to Mamie's urgent call, do make one wonder. Was he hoping this was a mild attack and that it could be concealed from the public? Could that be why he first directed Ann Whitman to have Murray Snyder tell the press that Ike was suffering from a digestive upset?

Mattingly's findings have resulted in a number of academics coming to share his opinion that Ike had suffered at least one heart attack and possibly two before his Denver attack in 1955, among them noted historian Robert W. Ferrell; Professor William Pickett, the author of the American Biographical History Series; and political scientist Robert Gilbert, author of the book *Mortal Presidency*.

Those who are of the opinion there were no previous heart attacks can also lay out a convincing argument. The most well-researched comes from Clarence Lasby, a University of Texas history professor. Lasby, a heart attack victim who has had two coronary bypass surgeries, is the author of the very comprehensive book *Eisenhower's Heart Attack: How Ike Beat Heart Disease and Held on to the Presidency*.

He surmises Dr. Leedham's claim of treating Ike for a heart attack may have been just braggadocio and he points out the lab work performed on Ike at Oliver Hospital was general tests.

As to the Key West EKG, Lasby found where a number of noted cardiologist had examined it and they did not agree with Mattingly's interpretation. Lasby also came across the fact that Ike had conducted meetings, although short in duration, with members of the Joint Chiefs of Staff. He also points to the mere fact that Ike was this active at this time, which was barely two weeks after the onset of the illness. If he had suffered a heart attack, this activity would have been at great odds with the standard treatment of a heart attack victim in 1949, which was extensive bed rest for the patient for a period of four to eight weeks.

Also, the impact of a heart attack on the patient's psychology in 1949 was much more significant than it is today. Emotional anxiety and a feeling of hopelessness among heart attack victims were common. Lasby could find no evidence of this kind of "psychic shock" in Ike's behavior during this time. Lasby also put great weight in reaching his conclusion on Ike's honor, integrity, and sense of duty, and that he would have never misled the American people about such an issue and perpetuated the deception for the rest of his life.

Lasby believes that Snyder misdiagnosed Ike's condition during those early morning hours and he did in fact believe he was dealing with a gastrointestinal problem. As to Snyder's bedside notes detailing his immediate diagnosis of a heart attack and his actions in response to that diagnosis, Lasby believes there is an overwhelming likelihood they were written well after the events in order to cover up Snyder's misdiagnosis.

Mattingly's suspicions about the 1953 illness being a heart attack would appear to be a reach, given the fact Ike broke 90 for the first time at Augusta National just three days after he took ill.

This was not the case in 1949. In Snyder's letter to Dr. Black that Mattingly suspected was "planted," Snyder stated that during Ike's second week at Key West he had practiced with his approach clubs one day, and during the last three afternoons, he had played nine holes of golf without undue fatigue, and certainly with no signs of exhaustion. But Cliff Roberts, in his book *The Augusta National Story*, provided this description of Ike when he arrived at Augusta National from Key West: "weak to the point of almost trembling." This hardly depicts a man capable of having played nine holes of golf on three consecutive days in the prior week at Key West.

Ike spent the latter part of November and half of December of 1956 at Augusta, preparing for his second term and getting in 14 rounds of golf. He may eventually have wished that he had never sought re-election, because the next four years would be rocky ones.

Preparations for his second-term inauguration, meetings with members of Congress from both sides of the aisle over his Mideast policy, and a state visit by King Saud of Saudi Arabia in a week, required Ike to start the year 1957 in Washington, instead of Augusta National, which had been his practice before his heart attack. He was also busy filling a number of key posts for his second administration. One of those posts was Ambassador to Great Britain and for that spot he selected fellow Augusta National member John Hay "Jock" Whitney. His new appointee had been born into tremendous wealth and then improved it through his management of a Wall Street investment firm. He was also a financial backer of over 30 Broadway shows and helped Hollywood Producer David O. Selznick with financial support in such highly profitable productions as *Rebecca* and *Gone With the Wind*.

In his second inaugural address, Ike called upon the country "to pay the high, full price of building a just world peace based on moral law." His address drew very positive reviews. *Time* magazine saw it this way: "...rarely before in U.S.

political history had the ideals and ideas of one man struck so responsive a chord among politicians, pundits and just plain people of generally divergent opinions." Two leading Democrats were just as impressed. Hubert Humphrey called it "magnificent." And Lyndon Johnson said Ike, "Had set forth goals and objectives with which every American will agree."

The ink was barely dry on all the praise his speech had received before there began to be signs of how tough a year it was going to be for Ike. The state visit of King Saud was of prime importance to him because he wanted to make sure the Saudis did not fall under Soviet influence. But getting King Saud to 1600 Pennsylvania Avenue would prove to be particularly challenging due to the King's prickly nature. Saud sent word that he would not come to Washington unless Ike agreed to greet him at the airport. It had always been presidential protocol that heads of state were greeted at the White House, but given the importance of good relations with Saudi Arabia to his Mideast policy, Ike grudgingly agreed to the request.

Ike had been afraid the King was going to show up with his harem, but that fear proved to be unfounded. But Saud and his entourage did bring something that almost overwhelmed Ike— the musky odor in their robes made it difficult for him to breathe when he was in their company.

But if Ike had a problem with Saud's group, the waiters at the White House did not. The Saudis brought a large amount of cash with them and passed out $50 and $100 bills to the wait staff freely during a state dinner held in Saud's honor. In the end, it was all worth it, because when Saud departed Washington, he was firmly in the United States' corner.

The weekend after the Saud visit, Ike tried to make up for lost time by making a quick trip to Augusta, but rain kept him inside the entire time. A week later, Ike was back in Georgia, making a return trip to the plantation of Treasury Secretary George Humphrey for some hunting. He also got in one round of golf at Glen Arven in Thomasville during his stay.

Ike's annual after-the-Masters trip to Augusta made big news because of a firing and a rumored resignation. The axe fell on the "First Caddie" Willie "Cemetery" Perteet. He was being replaced by Slim Jackson, the assistant caddie master at Augusta National. A shocked Cemetery told reporters, "I don't know what I have done wrong."

Augusta National Pro Ed Dudley did the firing, and although he was a great golf instructor, he came up a couple of clubs short in the public relations department. Dudley stated that the move was made because Cemetery, who was 51, was "getting a little decrepit."

The rumored resignation was that of Ike's recent host down at Thomasville, Treasury Secretary Humphrey. There were reports a big rift had developed between the two. In an attempt to quell the rumors, Humphrey accompanied Ike to Augusta. It had to be a long stay for Humphrey because he didn't play golf. Ike did coax him into taking a lesson from Ed Dudley. But for most of the trip, Humphrey's time was spent following Ike and his group around the course in a golf cart.

On this trip, Ike had barely settled into the Eisenhower Cabin when there was outcry from many for his return to Washington to handle a flare-up in the Middle East. As it seemed by all indications, Egypt and Syria were about to act on a plot to overthrow the 21-year-old ruler of Jordan, King Hussein.

Ike did not interrupt his vacation; however, he did interrupt the time off of a sizable number of Naval personnel. Most of the Sixth Fleet was on shore leave in ports on the western Mediterranean when he ordered the Fleet to sail for the coast of Jordan. In half a dozen French and Italian ports, U.S. shore patrols, aided by local police, marched into bars, hotels, and nightclubs and rounded up the Fleet's crews and in short order an impressive armada headed by two aircraft carriers and a 45,000-ton battleship were steaming for the coast of Jordan.

For the next few days, Augusta was a very busy place. At the Bon Air Hotel, Army Signal Corpsmen decoded incoming intelligence estimates and rushed them over to Augusta National. Courier planes dipped into nearby Bush Field with locked and guarded leather diplomatic pouches, also bound for Augusta National.

Ike stayed on top of the situation in his small office above the pro shop, putting in time there before and after his daily round, conferring with Secretary of State Dulles and the Pentagon by phone.

As soon as the Sixth Fleet appeared on the horizon off the Jordanian coast, the situation began to rapidly cool. In a matter of days, King Hussein declared the crisis had passed.

At the start of the summer, Ike played host to Japanese Prime Minister Nabusuhi Kishi at Burning Tree Golf Club. Ike got the day off to a good start by presenting Kishi with a set of Ben Hogan golf clubs tailored to fit the five-foot-four-inch prime minister. Kishi's first drive with his new driver was a dismal effort. Ike quickly offered him a mulligan. Kishi accepted the offer as if it were the most valuable foreign aid he had ever received. He then split the fairway with a nice drive. The match, which included Prescott Bush and another Japanese official, ended in a draw. Kishi did score a huge victory in talks after the round, when Ike agreed to withdraw the United States combat ground forces that had been occupying Japan since the end of World War II.

As the summer of 1957 wore on, Ike could hardly wait for Congress to adjourn so he could get away from Washington for a while. He wanted to return to Denver and the Cherry Hills Golf Club. He ran that idea by Dr. Mattingly. Fearing binge golfing in that high altitude would be too taxing on Ike's heart, Mattingly vetoed that idea.

It was then suggested that Newport Country Club in Newport, Rhode Island, might be a suitable alternative. Jim Hagerty was sent out on a reconnaissance mission and returned with a positive assessment of the course and Newport.

Based on the projected adjournment date of Congress, a date of August 14 was penciled in to begin the Newport golf holiday. This date turned out to be overly optimistic, however, as Congress's session ran three weeks longer than expected due to the lengthy debating and haggling over the first major Civil Rights legislation since Reconstruction.

The arguments over this legislation were heated and fervent. Black leaders such as Martin Luther King, Jr. and baseball great Jackie Robinson opposed it because they thought the legislation was too weak. Hard-line Southerners opposed the Bill because they thought it was too strong. Finally, on August

29th, the details of legislation had been hammered out and Senate members were ready to put the final measure to a vote; all except one, Senator Strom Thurmond of South Carolina.

The night the D-Day invasion commenced and Kay Summersby and Ike stood and watched the airborne units depart the airfield, Lt. Colonel Strom Thurmond most likely passed over their heads.

Thurmond was a Public Affairs officer and had been assigned to the 82nd Airborne. His mission was to assist the French in reestablishing local government once the Allies had secured an area. The glider Thurmond was aboard made a hard landing and many on board were injured, including Thurmond. Despite his injuries, Thurmond distinguished himself in the fierce fighting that began almost immediately after his glider came to a stop, as he was instrumental in getting his unit and other units around him to hook up and fight their way to safety.

Thirteen years later, Thurmond decided to take to the floor of the United States Senate in a one-man battle. He was a member of the Democratic Party at that time and he and his Southern Democratic colleagues had worked hard at watering down the Civil Rights Bill and all but Thurmond were satisfied they could now let the bill proceed toward passage.

Thurmond decided to start a filibuster. To invoke a filibuster, a senator must have the floor. Then the senator simply starts talking (and talking...). Once a filibuster starts, the complicated Senate rules make it extremely difficult for the rest of the Senate to do anything but listen, as long as the senator or senators conducting the filibuster have the floor.

Thurmond chose not to tell any of his fellow Senate colleagues what he planned to do. He took a number of steam baths to dehydrate his body during the day to decrease the need for urination and took to the podium on the Senate Floor at 8:54 p.m. on August 28. He hoped some of the other southern senators would rally behind him and join his effort, but a few hours into the filibuster it was clear he would receive no help.

Thurmond continued his one-man show throughout the night and into the morning. When Ike was advised about what was going on in the Senate, he issued a sarcastically tinged statement that he had expected a busy day. But since the Senate was tied up, he had decided to go to Burning Tree and play golf. With his cause hopelessly lost without support from other senators, Thurmond must have decided to go for the record for a Senate filibuster. The old mark was 22 hours and six minutes, set by Senator Wayne Morse in 1953. Thurmond finally stopped speaking at 9:12 p.m., establishing a new record that still stands today of 24 hours and 18 minutes. Shortly after Thurmond gave up the floor, the Senate approved the Civil Rights Bill by a vote of 60 to 15.

8

A BIG DRIVE BY THE SOVIETS

With the Civil Rights Bill now passed, Congress adjourned, and Ike was on the way to Newport for his vacation. He and Mamie arrived on September 4th and received a rousing reception. One local paper dubbed the scene "Ikemania." There were all sorts of welcoming festivities, and the First Couple was overwhelmed with gifts from the locals. One fisherman gave Ike a 27-pound lobster, and he was mortally offended when Ike failed to take it with him.

The First Couple stayed in a residence on the grounds of the Naval War College, where a small office was set up for Ike in one of its administrative buildings. The Newport Country Club was located across the bay from the War College, so the presidential yacht the Barbara Anne (named for one of Ike's granddaughters) was brought up from Washington to take him to the course each day.

The Newport Country Club had only 81 members but the

roster read like a Who's Who in United States society. It had been that way ever since the club was founded in 1893 by John Jacob Astor and Cornelius Vanderbilt and it soon earned a spot in America's golf history by hosting the first United States Open and the first United States Amateur Championship in 1895.

Located where it receives wind from both Narragansett Bay and the Atlantic Ocean, the course's original founders easily obtained what they desired, which was a rugged seaside links similar to those found in Scotland and England. In 1957, the course featured 132 sand traps, which was nearly three times the number Ike had to deal with at Augusta or Burning Tree, and it placed a premium on accuracy.

The fact the President of the United States was going to be playing there for almost a month had little effect on the Club. Ike had specifically requested nothing be changed on his account and his wishes were totally obeyed. The clubhouse remained in need of a coat of paint both inside and out and the badly-in-need-of-repair wicker furniture remained strewn around its porches.

The only indication the clubhouse was the President of the United States' golfing headquarters was a two-way radio station set up on the sun porch to allow "Golf Cart One" to stay in touch with the rest of the world. The cart had been flown up from Washington and was kept under lock and key at the nearby naval base between rounds. It was towed out to the course on a trailer each morning, approximately 30 minutes before Ike's arrival, by a gray Navy truck with "For Official Use Only" printed on its sides.

On the first day at the par-five opening hole, Ike ripped a

nice drive of about 225 yards. His second shot was also well struck and left him with a wedge to the green. He put that shot just five feet from the pin and then calmly stroked the putt into the hole for a birdie.

A number of residents from the estates around the course strolled down to watch Ike and his foursome that first day. One of the most pleasing to the eye in this group of spectators was a striking 28-year-old brunette, Jacqueline Kennedy. She and her senator husband had also decided to escape Washington and had rented an estate near the course for a lengthy vacation. JFK was also an interested onlooker that day, but he chose to be inconspicuous. He stood behind a utility pole in a clump of bushes to watch Ike and his group pass.

Ike's opening birdie was not a sign of good things to come. The wind, the sand traps, and par fours he called "par four and a halfs" took their toll on him. In fact, the opening birdie may have been the only good thing to happen to Ike on or off the course for the entire vacation.

In 1954, the Supreme Court had ruled in the Brown versus the Board of Education case that segregation in public schools was unconstitutional. The Court had ordered that desegregation was to take place with all deliberate speed. States in the South ran a delaying action after the ruling, which in most cases made deliberate speed more like snail speed.

One locale where deliberate speed and a federal court order had finally delivered black children to the steps of a previously all-white school was in Little Rock, Arkansas. Two days before Ike left Washington for Newport, Arkansas Governor Orval Faubus ordered the Arkansas National Guard out to prevent the integration plan from being implemented. Most observers assumed this was just saber-rattling by the Arkansas governor and after a few days of grandstanding, Faubus would back down. As the events in Little Rock began to unfold, there were calls by many for Ike to postpone his vacation and return to Washington until the crisis had been resolved. But Ike refused. He believed Faubus would soon have to realize there was no way out from a federal court order and that the White House was wherever he happened to be. He could deal with the crisis as effectively from Newport, just as he had done during the Middle East flare-up while he was at Augusta.

The situation in Little Rock quickly escalated. Segregationist sympathizers from other states began to pour into the city, and other Southern leaders publicly urged Faubus to keep up the stand. Faubus, however, was seeking a way out of the mess he had created but wanted to save face in the process. He sent a message to Ike through an intermediary, asking if he would be receptive to a telegram from Faubus that sought a meeting with him. Ike sent word back he would be receptive to such a request, on the condition that Faubus would stipulate in exact verbiage provided by Ike that he intended to comply with the order of the Federal Court.

Faubus' telegram arrived the next day just after Ike had teed off. Jim Hagerty took the telegram out to Ike, who was holing out on the first green. Ike reviewed the telegram in his golf cart. Although Faubus had modified the verbiage Ike had stipulated he use, Ike made no comment on the changes, and he directed Hagerty to go ahead and set up the meeting. Faubus arrived from Arkansas 48 hours later, and he and Ike met for an hour and 20 minutes on the morning of September 14. Unfortunately, when the meeting concluded, Ike had one impression of what had been agreed upon and Faubus had another. Ike thought Faubus had agreed to go back to Arkansas and use the National Guard to enforce the court order, not to prevent it. Faubus thought they had agreed only to meet again after lunch. When he showed up after lunch, he was told Ike had already left for the golf course. Faubus returned to Arkansas, and the situation only grew worse.

Ike was now taking a beating in the press both at home and abroad as pictures of mob scenes in Little Rock were contrasted with pictures of him walking off the 18th green. Many of Ike's advisors were now emphatically urging him to get off the course and go back to Washington to deal with the problem. But Ike was stubborn and he stuck to his belief that he could deal with a problem just as effectively away from Washington.

On Monday, September 23, Ike was on the way to the course when he was called back because of new developments in Arkansas. Faubus had pulled the National Guard out of Little Rock. The black children had entered the school that morning, but shortly thereafter, they had to be slipped out of the building under police guard because a mob of segregationists had practically surrounded the school and were threatening violence. Ike detested the idea of having to call out federal troops to enforce the law. He issued a strong statement warning that was what he fully intended to do if the situation continued. He expressed the hope that "the American sense of justice and fair play would prevail." He then ordered all persons engaged in the disturbances to cease and desist.

Ike's statement fell on deaf ears, and the following morning, he received an urgent message from the mayor of Little Rock that the situation had reached critical mass and mob rule was about to ensue. Ike had no other choice but to act. He ordered out the 101st Airborne Division, and by sundown, one thousand troops were on the ground in Little Rock and in thorough control of the situation. Ike returned to Washington that afternoon and addressed the nation that evening from the Oval Office to explain his actions.

The next day, Ike resumed his vacation in Newport, getting in four more rounds of golf as Little Rock cooled down rapidly. He ended his vacation and returned to Washington on October 1st. On the fourth, Ike sent a message over to Richard Nixon's office asking his Vice President if he thought it was safe to play golf, and if so, could he join him at Burning Tree that afternoon? Nixon answered affirmatively to both questions. It would be Ike's last chance to relax before another huge event that caused the editors of *Life* magazine to warn, "the world might be at a turning point."

While Nixon and Ike had been playing Burning Tree that fateful Friday, half a world away, the Soviet Union was teeing up a ball of its own. It was about the size of a beach ball and weighed 184 pounds. It would be propelled into flight by several huge cylinders filled with a combination of liquid oxygen and kerosene. That evening, in what would have to be called the original "October Surprise," the Soviets pulled off one of the biggest shots of the 20th century when they sent Sputnik, the Earth's first artificial satellite, into orbit.

Sputnik was an event that created a state of shock and

dismay in the country. An editorial cartoon by Herb Block of *The Washington Post* put a golf spin on the historic occasion. The cartoon depicted Russian Premier Nikita Khrushchev prancing gleefully with a golf club (a driver) raised high in his hand and the Sputnik satellite sailing off into orbit. America was stunned. It looked as though in the space race, the Russians were starting the back nine while the United States was still on the first tee. A state of near-panic ensued, as many Americans now believed it was only a matter of time before the USSR would have the capability to pelt the United States with nuclear weapons launched from space. Physicist Edward Teller, a key member of the Manhattan Project team that developed the atomic bomb and the father of the hydrogen bomb, said the country had lost "a battle more important and greater than Pearl Harbor." A month after the launch of Sputnik, Ike took a trip up to West Point for a reunion of his class and then watched the Army football team run the score up on an outclassed Colgate squad, 55-7. Soon after the game was over, Ike learned the Soviets were running up the score on the United States. They had put a second Sputnik in orbit, and this one carried a passenger, a dog named Laika.

Ike refused to panic; he knew the Soviets were still years behind the United States militarily. They had shown they could put an aluminum ball into space, but in almost every other category, they were woefully under-clubbed.

In mid-November, Ike sought a brief respite from the furor in Washington and took off to Augusta for a four-day stay. When he arrived there, he was greeted by a group of black civil rights protestors who were picketing the entrance to the club as he entered the grounds.

Back in Washington 11 days later, Ike was hosting the King of Morocco at a ceremony that included a parade through Washington. It concluded in the middle of the afternoon and Ike returned to the White House and went to bed immediately because he felt chilled. Dr. Snyder checked his blood pressure and pulse and then placed a hot-water bottle at his feet.

After an hour, Ike got up, had a bite to eat and then went to the Oval Office. When he sat down at his desk, he experienced a sense of dizziness and found it impossible to pick up a piece of paper. He dropped his pen and failed on three attempts to retrieve it. Ann Whitman then appeared in his office. She had noticed when he walked by her moments before that he appeared to be leaning to one side. When she attempted to speak with him, his reply came out as gibberish. Whitman then summoned Dr. Snyder and he and another staffer helped Ike back to his White House bedroom.

A neurologist from Walter Reed was summoned and he concluded after examining Ike that he had suffered a mild stroke. While the doctors were conferring on what to do next, Ike was already showing improvement. Unobserved by them, he had gotten out of bed, put on his robe and walked down to Mamie's room to discuss the State Dinner that was to be held for the King of Morocco that evening. When Sergeant Moaney reported Ike's whereabouts to the doctors, they quickly got him back into bed.

Unfortunately for Ike, Jim Hagerty was in Europe. Murray Snyder, his assistant who had been called onto handle Ike's heart attack, had recently moved over to the Defense Department to head its Department of Public Affairs. So the task of informing the press about Ike's stroke fell to Ann Wheaton, Snyder's replacement. Although she had extensive experience as a press representative for a number of high profile Republicans, Wheaton had only been in her post a short time and she stumbled hard in her first major performance before a frenzied White House press corps. She had trouble with her statement as to Ike's condition and in answering the White House press corps' follow-up questions. So much trouble in fact that the United Press International initially reported that Ike had suffered a "heart attack of the brain."

Ike bounced back quickly and after spending several days in Gettysburg recuperating, he returned to the White House and went back to work. On that first day back, he met with the cabinet, worked on his correspondence, and met with several staff members. Later in the afternoon, he went outside to practice with his 8-iron for a while. After a good workout with that club, he decided to work on his chipping. In just a few strokes, he came down with the most dreaded golf disease known to man —"the shanks."

A few days later, on December 6, the United States Space Program shanked a shot as well. Rushing to get up an answer to Sputnik, America's first attempt to launch a space satellite exploded just two seconds after lift-off. It had been that kind of year for Ike.

On the last day of January 1958, the United States finally got its first satellite into orbit. The next day Ike flew to Augusta to play his first golf since his stroke. But his visit came in a patch of bad weather. On the first day he got in 15 holes before high winds and storm clouds forced him inside. On his second and last day, he could play only four holes, as the high winds persisted and the temperature was plummeting.

Two weeks later, Ike took some time off and made another trip to George Humphrey's estate at Thomasville, Georgia, to do some quail hunting and play a few rounds of golf at Glen Arven Country Club. Again he found the Georgia weather inhospitable; it was unusually cold, forcing him to stay indoors most of the visit. This surprised the press because on past vacations he had not usually allowed bad weather to interfere with his activities. They were also amazed that there was not the usual flow of press releases from Jim Hagerty to give the impression Ike was doing some work on the trip. Nor was there the constant shuttle of cabinet members, flying in and out for quick conferences, which had almost always been the case during Ike's other lengthy stays away from the White House. The press speculated that Ike was slowing down and that the stroke in November had been a harder punch than originally reported, and combined with the heart attack, his age of 67, and the strains of the presidency, Ike was simply running out of steam.

Ike did not come out to hunt until his eighth day in Thomasville. The press corps went into a frenzy when he finally appeared and surrounded him like a pack of hunting dogs that had just cornered their prey. Ike snapped at them, "It's really something when you have to make this a news event to write about." In just a few minutes, however, they had their story. They took Ike to task on gun safety. Ike had made some gestures with his 20-gauge shotgun without seeming to care what direction it was pointed, and when Ike was seated in the horse-drawn hunting cart, he had his hand over its muzzle.

After reading about the incident in a newspaper a couple of days later, Ike told his host George Humphrey the following story:

"There was an old mountaineer in front of a country store leaning on a muzzle-loading musket. A young fellow from the city walked up to him and said, 'It's always the gun that isn't loaded that goes off and kills someone.' And the mountaineer replied, 'In that case, we're perfectly safe because this one is loaded.'"

The dust-up over gun safety didn't hold a candle to what was coming next. Mamie had undergone a hysterectomy the previous August. Since the surgery, she had not been herself and she was upset over the fact she had also picked up a few pounds in all the wrong places. During their Thomasville trip, Mamie decided she wanted to indulge herself with a two-week stay at the famed haven for a woman's well-being: the Elizabeth Arden Arizona Maine Chance beauty ranch near Phoenix. The ranch offered a full range of beauty treatments and fitness and diet programs.

It had been kicked around that Mamie should take a commercial flight to Phoenix, but that idea had been nixed because of her extreme fear of flying. Ike decided he would take her out there on the Columbine III and then return to Washington. When the news of this trip hit the media, it stirred up quite a firestorm over its cost to the taxpayer.

The residents of Phoenix, however, appeared to be very happy the First Couple was paying their area a visit. On February 23, a crowd of 25,000 showed up at the airport to greet them. Ike and Mamie created quite a traffic jam because the couple split up into two different motorcades. Mamie's headed off for the beauty ranch while Ike's headed for the Paradise Valley Golf Club, so he could get in a round before heading back to Washington.

By the time Ike left Phoenix, the uproar from Democrats and the press over the trip was ferocious. But Ike soon received some well-needed support from what had to be considered an unlikely source: former president Harry Truman, who remained one of the leading voices of the Democratic Party. Truman believed there was no reason for anyone to criticize Ike for escorting Mamie to Arizona in the presidential plane at government expense and concluded his thoughts on the matter with this statement: "Whatever the President sees fit to do for the welfare of his family, he should be allowed to without a lot of people jumping on him."

For her return trip to Washington, Mamie, who was now five pounds lighter, was again aboard Ike's plane. During her two-week stay, the Columbine III was flown to the Lockheed Aircraft maintenance facility at Ontario, California, for a six-month checkup. On its return trip to Washington, it stopped in Phoenix to pick up Mamie.

In late 1957, the United States' long economic boom had burned out and the country had slipped into recession. Ike's vacations and golf came under increasing fire. Pulitzer-Prize-winning reporter and Washington Bureau Chief and columnist for *The New York Times* James Reston wrote this in an editorial:

...Protected from criticism more than most Presidents, he is responding more willfully and stubbornly to the criticism that is now beginning to appear. But the main change is not in him but in the mood of the country. It will tolerate absenteeism for golf, or even trips to beauty farms, when everybody is working, but when 5,000,000 are unemployed and business receipts are down, people are more attentive and critical.

Ike went to Augusta for a weekend in late March. In mid-April, he made his usual after-the-Masters-Tournament trip. This stay was just for a couple of days due to other commitments. Two days after he returned to Washington, Jim Wright, a 36-year-old freshman Democratic congressman from Texas, who would later become Speaker of the House, made headlines when he suggested Ike visit small towns and see their need for public works projects instead of visiting golf courses. Ironically, Wright was not into golf at that time, but after he became a leader in his party, he hosted a golf tournament in his home district as a political fund-raiser that was such a stellar event that even House Republicans took part in it.

Ike wasn't the only member of his administration who was encountering problems as a result of his travels. Two weeks after Ike returned from Augusta, Vice President Nixon paid a visit to Venezuela. During a public ceremony he was spat on and later his limousine was surrounded and pelted with rocks and bottles by a mob of anti-American demonstrators. Nixon and his party eventually made it to the safety of the U.S. Embassy compound. Ike dispatched two companies of Marines, two companies of the 101st Airborne Division, and a carrier group to the area to stand by in case they were needed to cover Nixon's departure. Nixon, with the aid of the Venezuelan military, made it to the airport safely the next afternoon, and he departed without incident. Ike was kept apprised of the situation that day by walkie-talkie, as he played a round at Burning Tree.

9

CLIFF'S LETTER

July 5, 1958, was a red-letter day for Ike at the Gettysburg Country Club. He teed off shortly after seven in the morning. Three-and-a-half hours later, he rolled in a long birdie putt on the 18th green for a score of 79. This was one of only a handful of times that he ever broke 80.

Ike's good showing on the course that day was probably aided by the presence on the front nine of one of his most favorite people in the world, David Eisenhower, his grandson. David's experiences at the course with Ike during his formative years would be quite different from those of his father, John Sheldon Doud Eisenhower.

Ike and Mamie had two sons. The first born was Doud Dwight Eisenhower. Nicknamed Ikky, his death at age three from scarlet fever was the greatest sorrow of the couple's lives. John was born 20 months after Ikky's death.

In the early 1930s, Ike was assigned to the office of the Assistant Secretary of War in Washington, D.C. He occasionally played a round on Sunday afternoon at the cow pasture-like course at the Old Soldiers Home. Ike's skill level on the course at that time was barely past that of a beginner.

John often accompanied him and shared a bit of that experience in his book about his father titled *Strictly Personal*: "Dad would make a tee out of wet sand, and then take a big, powerful swing that produced a horrendous slice. Often, at this point, the air would be punctuated with expletives."

Growing up as a typical Army kid, the family's frequent moves placed John in a number of different schools in both the United States and abroad. His final years of high school were spent living with his uncle Edgar in Tacoma. Edgar offered to pay for his education if he would go to law school and then join his practice after graduation. But John did not think working with his uncle would be a good fit. He opted instead to attend West Point. His class graduated during the week of D-Day and he had a long and distinguished career in the Army.

In the summer of 1951, when he was twenty-eight years old, John used some leave time to visit Ike at NATO headquarters in Paris. Soon after his arrival, he played a round of golf with his father. John's skill level at golf at that point was comparable to his father's at the Old Soldiers Home course 20 years earlier and it was a very long afternoon for him. Two Augusta National members, Barry Leithead and Cliff Roberts, were the other two players in the foursome that day in Paris. After the round, Roberts pulled John aside.

He told him he was certainly no professional, but had been

around the game long enough that he believed he could be of some assistance. John accepted his offer of help and the two went to the practice range. Roberts' golf advice must have been on par with the advice he gave his Wall Street clients as after John's session with Roberts, his ball-striking ability showed tremendous improvement, making the ten more rounds he would play with his father before departing Paris much more enjoyable.

After the Paris experience, John played golf somewhere between the casual and serious category and he played often with his father while he was President. But he certainly never gave the game the weight Ike did, nor did there ever appear to be any pressure from his father for him to do so. This was not the case, however, for John's son David.

The day Ike shot his stellar round of 79 at Gettysburg was also the start of a new chapter in David's life and it would be one he would not enjoy as it was on that fateful morning the 10-year-old teed it up with his grandfather for the first time.

David once described the experience of being grandson to the "First Golfer" in an interview:

My grandfather really took this game seriously–I was really force-fed golf. I was required to be on the tee and in full uniform for inspection at the stated hour. Grandfather really got disgusted at those shots which would go booming out into the trees. He couldn't hit very far himself, and he was a great believer in hitting a nice safe shot in the middle of the fairway. My shots sort of outran their supplies, so to speak.

Once, at the farm at Gettysburg, something else outran David, and that was his pony. It bolted away from him, and he had to chase it down. Before he could catch it, the little runaway galloped right across Ike's cherished practice putting green, just as Ike was showing it off to a visitor.

While force-feeding David golf, Ike would tell his young charge that one day he was going to be thankful his grandfather had taught him the game. But as hard as Ike tried to fan the flames, golf would always be in a take-it-or-leave-it category with David with the most emphasis on the latter.

A team of six Secret Service agents usually protected Ike when he was on the golf course. Several would carry golf bags that included a couple of clubs, along with a submachine gun and a rifle or two. A few days after his sub-80 round at Gettysburg, Ike was in Ottawa, Canada, for meetings with Canadian officials. During the visit, he played a round of golf with several of his hosts at the Ottawa Hunt and Golf Club.

As Ike was playing the back nine, his Secret Service detail went on high alert. A taxi cab driver reported to police that he had dropped two men off on the edge of the Ottawa Hunt and Golf Club's property. The cab driver stated one of the men was carrying a case that could have contained a rifle and he had seen what appeared to be the butt of a pistol in the other man's pocket.

When Canadian Prime Minister John Diefenbaker learned of the report, he left his office and rushed out to the course. Ike's group had just reached the 14th hole when Diefenbaker arrived. He was shocked to learn Ike had yet to be advised of the situation. He sought out James Rowley, the chief of Ike's

Secret Service detail, and recommended Ike be taken from the course. He also offered to provide the excuse that he had something important to discuss with him. Rowley declined the suggestion. He told the Prime Minister his men had combed the area and had found no sign of the two men. A few minutes later, Rowley did advise Ike of the situation on the 15th tee, and Ike, without hesitation, said he was going to continue to play. The news had no effect on his game. He and his partner went on to win the backside and take a $15 wager from their opponents.

Sherman Adams was not only Ike's Chief of Staff, he was the administration's official enforcer when it came to malfeasance or even the appearance of wrongdoing. His actions in this area were quick and punitive, and he was perceived to be the "Mr. Clean" of the Eisenhower Administration.

Another aspect of Adams' life was that he was a notorious spendthrift. When he traveled to Denver following Ike's heart attack, he declined the use of a military plane and flew coach instead. He reused stationary and brown-bagged his lunch. He told a *U.S. News and World Report* correspondent in 1957 that until recently he had been wearing a suit that had been made by a Boston tailor in 1918.

Ironically, in the summer of 1958, clothing would be at the center of Adams' downfall in the biggest scandal of Ike's presidency. To the surprise of almost everyone, Democrats in Congress charged that Adams had accepted free hotel rooms and personal gifts from a New Hampshire businessman named Bernard Goldfine. It was also charged that Adams had made a call on Goldfine's behalf to the Securities and Exchange

Commission. Adams admitted making the call, but he stated it was done only to expedite a matter concerning Goldfine, not to bring influence to bear.

Adams appeared before a Congressional committee in an attempt to explain his actions but the situation continued to spiral downward. It was soon established Adams had stayed in hotels on Goldfine's tab while White House Chief of Staff at least 20 times. The list of the gifts Adams had accepted was produced: liquor, an Oriental rug, and an expensive coat for his wife, which would become the marquee item of the scandal. Republican Party leaders and Ike's friends wanted him to get rid of Adams. But Ike wanted desperately to try to keep him.

In the heat of the Adams uproar, Cliff Roberts' behind-the-scenes role in the Eisenhower Administration suddenly became big news. The day the scandal first hit the papers, Roberts had made some phone calls about Mr. Goldfine and had concluded that this matter was going to be big trouble for Ike. When the scandal was nearing the boiling point, Roberts sent Adams a letter urging him to resign. Adams' secretary opened the letter and read it. Instead of passing the letter on to Adams, she sent it to Ann Whitman with a note asking if it would be appropriate for Whitman to send the letter back to Roberts.

Since she was aware from other communications that Roberts had gone to Europe, Whitman chose not to send the letter back and placed it in her desk. Several days later, a reporter called Ann, telling her word about the letter was circulating and Ike was going to resign from Augusta National because of it. Whitman denied the Augusta story. She then told

Ike what had happened. According to Whitman, he mildly rebuked her.

Whitman met with Roberts when he returned from Europe and told him she had his letter and that Adams had not yet seen it. She said he was angry, but did not attempt to upbraid her.

When Roberts got back to his New York office, he was contacted by the press about the letter. He told them any communication he had had with Mr. Adams was purely personal. And that Adams must have received a bushel basket full of letters and he did not see why anybody would care what his said.

Soon after the letter flap, Roberts and fellow "gang member" Pete Jones met face to face with Ike to persuade him to dump Adams. Roberts recalled years later he let Jones do most of the talking at the meeting because he was the better of the two at presenting a convincing verbal argument. Shortly after their meeting, Ike started the ball rolling on Adams' departure.

In his book, *In the Arena*, Richard Nixon described how Adams' ouster unfolded. Nixon was on vacation with his family at the Greenbrier Resort in West Virginia, where he had been getting some lessons from Sam Snead on his short game, when Ike sent word he needed him back in Washington. When Nixon got back to the District, he and Ike went to Burning Tree for a round and to discuss the Adams problem. It was decided Nixon and Republican Party Chairman Meade Alcorn would meet with Adams at the White House and advise him that Ike wanted him to resign. In their meeting, Adams refused to believe what Nixon and Alcorn had told him and stated he wanted to hear it directly from Ike. Adams then went into the Oval Office to speak with Ike. The meeting lasted only a few minutes, and Adams agreed to resign. As Nixon was leaving the White House minutes after the resolution had been reached, he noticed Ike out on the South Lawn hitting 8-iron shots.

Ike took his 1958 summer vacation from late August to late September back in Newport. His summer vacation quarters were moved to the Newport Country Club side of the bay so the presidential yacht was not needed for golf transport on this trip. Ike played 20 rounds at the Newport Country Club. He had to make a couple of quick trips back to Washington to handle problems but they were not of the magnitude of the Little Rock crisis of the prior year.

In March of 1958, the United States Golf Association and the Royal and Ancient Golf Club of St. Andrews announced they were going to sponsor a biennial international amateur tournament that would feature four-man teams and the inaugural event would take place at St. Andrews in early October of that year. In May, it was announced that in Ike's honor, the event would be called the Eisenhower Cup.

In the tournament, Australia took the championship in a playoff against the United States team, but there was another happening at St. Andrews that week that outranked the golf played on the Old Course. And that was the return to St. Andrews of Bobby Jones, who captained the United States team in the competition.

Ike and several members of his administration had approached Bobby Jones about his interest in serving the administration in an official capacity but Jones had always declined, citing his ever-increasing problem with lack of mobility because of his spinal disease. His most recent rejection had been to Richard Nixon's request that he serve on the Physical Fitness Commission. When he was asked to captain the United States team in the competition named for one of his best friends and to return to his favorite course in the world, Jones decided it was something he really wanted to do and he wasn't going to allow his physical problems to get in the way.

Jones was St. Andrews' cherished adopted son, so loved and so idolized by the town that he was as much at home with its citizenry as he was with the populace of his hometown of Atlanta. It was not love at first sight, however, when Jones made his first appearance at the Old Course in the 1921 British Open as a much heralded 19-year-old prodigy. He loathed what he saw. He did not look upon the course that was the cradle of golf as a treasure. Instead, he viewed it as a barren pasture laden with hidden horrors and his play reflected it. He started that Open Championship with two fair rounds. But in the third round the wind began to howl and the Old Course dismantled Jones' game. He shot 46 on the front side. He started the back with a double-bogey at 10. Then at the par three 11th, he put his tee shot in that hole's infamous greenside Hill Bunker. When after three shots he had still not extracted his ball from that bunker, Jones picked it up and put it in his pocket and stormed backed to the clubhouse. On the way, he tore up his scorecard and tossed it into an estuary of the Eden River.

Jones returned to St. Andrews for the Walker Cup in 1926

with a much different outcome, not losing a match and spurring the United States team to a 6 ½ to 5 ½ victory.

He was back at the Old Course the following year for the British Open and held the galleries spellbound with his play, walking away with a six-stroke victory and the hearts of the St. Andrews faithful, who swarmed around him as if he were one of their own when his final putt dropped. At the awards ceremony, Jones further endeared himself to the citizens of St. Andrews when he said this: "Nothing would make me happier than to take home your trophy, but I cannot. It was played for here 30 years before I was born. Please honor me by allowing it to be kept here at the Royal and Ancient Club where it belongs."

St. Andrews' already enormous affection for Jones seemed to double when he won the British Amateur there in 1930, the first leg of his historic Grand Slam. Six years later, in 1936, Jones stopped by on his way to attend the Olympics in Berlin to play a round. After he teed off, word spread through the town he was back and by the time he made the turn a gallery of over 2,000 had come out to see their hero play the Old Course one more time.

Later, in his autobiography, *Golf Is My Game*, Jones wrote this about St. Andrews:

The more I studied the Old Course, the more I loved it, and the more I loved it, the more I studied it, so that I came to feel that it was for me the most favorite meeting ground possible for an important match. Truly, if I had to select one course upon which to play the match of my life, I should have selected the Old Course.

Jones' captaincy of the American team in the Eisenhower Cup led to one of the most moving moments in the annals of sports, on par with Lou Gehrig's farewell speech at Yankee Stadium.

During the course of the event at a packed Younger Hall in St. Andrews, a ceremony was held in which Jones was made an honorary freeman of the Borough of St. Andrews, the first American to be so honored since Benjamin Franklin. The provost of St. Andrews, Robert Leonard, a friend of Jones of long standing, made the presentation and declared to a roar of approval from the 1700 people who had jammed the old hall that Jones was, "The most distinguished golfer of this age...I might say of all times."

Jones, despite his physical problems, gamely made his way to the podium. The spirits of the citizens in the hall must have dipped to see their hero in this condition. The young golfer with the great game and Hollywood looks, who had captured their hearts with his performances at the Old Course over a quarter century before, was now struggling just to walk.

Jones rose to the occasion one more time at St. Andrews. Herbert Warren Wind, noted golf writer, was in the hall that evening and provided this account for *Sports Illustrated*:

Jones spoke for 10 minutes, beautifully and movingly. He told his friends in the audience, "You people have sensitivity and an ability to extend cordially in ingenious ways." He said of the

Old Course, "The more you study it, the more you love it, the more you study it." He said near the end of his talk, "I could take out of my life experiences everything except St. Andrews and I'd still have a rich and full life." He left the stage and got into an electric golf cart. As he drove down the center aisle to leave, the whole hall spontaneously burst into the old Scottish song, "Will Ye No' Come Back Again?" So honestly heartfelt was this reunion for Jones and the people of St. Andrews (and for everyone) that it was 10 minutes before many who attended were able to speak with a tranquil voice.

Ike closed out his golf in 1958 with a 10-day stay at Augusta National over Thanksgiving. Domestic and foreign issues and bad weather combined to produce a long golf-less spell for Ike at the beginning of 1959. He again returned to George Humphrey's place in Thomasville, Georgia, for a winter vacation. But the weather was so uncooperative he cut the trip short and returned to Washington. Two weeks later, Ike made a trip to Acapulco to meet with Mexican President Lopez Mateos. He planned to stop off at Augusta National for a few days on the return trip, but the Georgia weather again proved to be uncooperative, and he cancelled those plans.

After Ike's heart attack and later the stroke, Dr. Snyder wanted to keep an even closer eye on him to try to keep him as calm as possible; his actions, however, would lead one to wonder if he was not actually an impediment to Ike's well being. In a round during Ike's first vacation to Newport in 1957, he missed the fairway on one of the holes with his drive and the ball came to rest underneath a low-hanging tree limb. Ike squeezed his way under the limb and hit a perfect punch shot back into the fairway. But as he was exiting out from under the limb, he scraped his head against it. When he took his hat off and put his hand to his head, it came away with blood on the fingertips. Ike called Snyder over and asked for some disinfectant and a Band-Aid. Snyder's medical bag contained neither. A Secret Service agent had to be dispatched back to the clubhouse to get a first aid kit.

Ike, like many golfers, had a number of idiosyncrasies when he played a round. One was you didn't make any boastful comments about how well you were doing for fear it would trigger a reversal of fortune. During a round in 1958 at Newport, a Snyder comment almost caused Ike to blow a fuse. When Ike canned a birdie putt at the third hole, Snyder enthusiastically commented, "My god, two pars and a birdie on the first three holes!" Ike lividly responded to his comment, "Keep your ##&!!## mouth shut, Howard." Ike hit a poor drive on the next hole which led to a double bogey and he growled at his caddie as he walked off the green, "Too ##&&!!# bad you have to have people around who shoot off their mouths."

Soon after Ike arrived at Augusta for his 1959 after-the-Masters vacation, Snyder triggered a total Ike meltdown. It was one of those instantaneous rage events that had peppered Ike's life. And it occurred on the 17th hole, a piece of real estate that anyone close to Ike should have known to be extra careful about when they were with him in this area.

Each year during the Masters television broadcast viewers are reminded about Ike's close association with the Augusta National as a result of comments made about the Eisenhower Cabin and a certain pine tree on the 17th hole. No account of

Ike's involvement with Augusta National would be complete without addressing the latter. This pine tree was the one thing he could not stand about the course. It stands guard on the left side of the fairway, approximately 150 yards from the 17th tee, and it caused Ike more trouble than any Democrat ever did. His drives typically started out to the left and then would fade back to the right. The pine's position was just before the distance at which Ike's ball would start to bend back to the right. Countless times, Ike's rounds were tarnished when his tee shot at the 17th caromed off one of the tree's branches. So frequent was this occurrence, the tree was eventually dubbed by the gang as "Eisenhower's Pine."

On the day Snyder triggered the meltdown, Ike had had a good front nine but the wheels had started to come off on the back side. He double-bogeyed the par-five 15th and bogeyed the par-three 16th. Snyder was always concerned about Ike's blood pressure shooting up, which was probably why his comment that resulted in Ike's coming completely unhinged was voiced. On this day, Ike had escaped the clutches of the Eisenhower Pine. What drop in blood pressure he experienced from the tee shot was quickly negated when his approach shot found the bunker that guards the right front side of the 17th green.

Ike made a poor explosion shot from the bunker and perhaps in an attempt to keep Ike's temper in check, Snyder yelled out, "Fine shot!" But his comment had the reverse effect as Ike exploded. He shouted back at Snyder, "Fine shot, hell, you son of a bitch!" and slung his sand wedge at Snyder. Unfortunately for Dr. Snyder, at his age, he couldn't dodge and he couldn't jump, so the club struck him in the shins. Luckily for him, only the shaft hit him, not the heavy clubface. Ike's apology was an, "Oh pardon me!" It is not known how long it took Snyder to shake off the effect of the incident. But Ike seemed to put it behind him quickly, because he parred the last hole.

10

IN NEED OF A MULLIGAN

I n the summer of 1959, Ike decided that it might be time to invite Soviet Premier Nikita Khrushchev to the United States. He instructed the State Department to issue an invitation, provided there was progress at a foreign ministers' conference that was attempting to deal with a number of critical problems between the two superpowers.

The State Department dropped the ball and invited Khrushchev without mentioning the condition that Ike wanted progress at the foreign ministers' meeting first. Khrushchev quickly accepted, and Ike had no other choice but to honor the invitation with no strings attached.

The United States' allies were caught off guard by the announcement, so Ike chose to make a quick trip to Europe before Khrushchev's scheduled mid-September visit to ease the anxiety of the leaders in Great Britain, West Germany, and France.

The first stop was Great Britain and a meeting with British

Prime Minister Harold Macmillan. While in London, Ike stayed at Winfield House, the estate Woolworth heiress Betty Hutton had donated to the United States after World War II for use as the American ambassador to Great Britain's official residence. Ike found the huge back lawn of the estate too inviting to resist. He directed poor old Dr. Snyder to mark off 150 yards. And then to stand there and serve as a target so Ike and Jock Whitney, the Augusta National member whom Ike had appointed Ambassador to Great Britain, could practice some irons shots. Snyder managed to survive the session without getting struck.

From Great Britain it was on to West Germany to meet with their leader, Konrad Adenauer, and then to France for talks with Charles De Gaulle. After stroking his Allies about his forthcoming talks with Khrushchev, Ike decided he wanted to take some strokes of his own, and he made a side trip to Scotland.

In 1945, the owner of one of Scotland's most famous castles, Culzean, donated it to the country's National Trust. Designed in the 18th century, the grand, three-story castle is located on a cliff top on Scotland's Ayrshire Coast. There was one proviso attached to the donation by its owner and that was in consideration for his efforts in securing victory in World War II, Ike would be granted use of the castle's third-floor apartment for life. With the Turnberry Golf Course, a future site of four British Opens, located just down the road from the castle, Ike thought it would be a good time for a short layover.

Before leaving Paris, Ike placed calls to gang members Bill Robinson and Pete Jones in New York. He requested that they join him on the links in Scotland. They both dropped what plans they had and scrambled to make flight arrangements that would allow them to arrive in time to play the next day.

Ike flew on to Scotland to get in a round that afternoon. He arrived at the castle, changed clothes, and headed over to the Turnberry Golf Club. Boosted by a birdie on a par five, he shot a very respectable 42 on the front side. His whirlwind travel schedule, and possibly his 69-year-old body, began to tell on him on the backside, as the wheels on his game began to wobble a bit. But he still reached the 18th tee needing only a double-bogey six to break 90.

Ike made the final hole a real adventure. He sculled his drive, and it went nowhere. He then hit a decent recovery fairway wood shot, but followed it with a poor iron shot that ended up in a greenside bunker. His explosion shot just made it onto the green, but he managed to two-putt for a six and a score of 89. Ike's play with Robinson and Jones on Saturday and Sunday was said to have been more solid, as he was reported to have posted scores in the mid-80s both days.

Khrushchev arrived in Washington shortly after Ike's return from Scotland, and they had some preliminary discussions at the White House. Khrushchev then embarked on a tour of the country, visiting New York City, Iowa farms, and Hollywood. He was bitterly disappointed in California when his request to visit Disneyland was turned down for security reasons. His pain over that denial, however, was soothed over when he was afforded the opportunity to meet Marilyn Monroe. She was quite a sight to behold, since she had been instructed to wear the tightest-fitting dress she owned for the good of Soviet-American relations.

Khrushchev wrapped up his 10-day visit by returning to Washington. He and Ike were helicoptered to Camp David for two days of intense talks. Ike also took the Soviet leader over to his farm at Gettysburg. On the way out of Washington, Ike gave him an aerial view of Burning Tree. Khrushchev would later write about that moment, stating, "We flew over a big green field where he told me he played golf. He asked me whether I liked the sport, and I didn't have the slightest idea what it was all about. He told me it was a very healthy sport."

Despite neither leader being up to par—Khrushchev had trouble sleeping during his tour, and Ike was fighting a severe cold he had caught on the links in Scotland—the spirit of their talks raised world expectations dramatically over the possibility of peaceful coexistence between the two superpowers. Ike agreed to visit the USSR in the summer of 1960. Khrushchev left the United States all aglow and went back to Russia and immediately began to plan for Ike's visit. He planned to spare no expense to make his newfound friend feel welcome when he visited his country. On a magnificent pine bluff overlooking a lake, he was going to build a grand house for Ike's use during his stay. His other good American friend, Llewellyn Thompson, the United States Ambassador to the Soviet Union, had also convinced him that not having a golf course in the Soviet Union hurt the country's prestige. Preparations were underway to build a course and have it ready in time for Ike to play when he arrived. There were even reports that Khrushchev was going to take some lessons so he could play a few holes with Ike during his visit.

The cold Ike had picked up in Scotland lingered and two

weeks after Khrushchev had departed, he decided that warm air, sunshine, and golf was the prescription he needed. Unfortunately, Augusta National was not scheduled to open up for another month, so he opted for a healing trip to Palm Springs, California, instead. But after an eight-day stay, he returned to Washington still with a cold. The malady continued to persist, and on October 20th, Ike called Cliff Roberts at his office in New York and asked if he could open up Augusta National early for him. Roberts agreed to do it. He put together just enough staff to pull it off with an assist from Sergeant Moaney, who did all the cooking for the group out of the kitchen at the Eisenhower Cabin.

Ike stayed for four days. Roberts described the four days as the worst stretch of weather Ike ever experienced at Augusta, each of the days being cloudy and cool with occasional showers. Ike was undaunted by the elements, however, and took the cure. He played 18 holes the first day, 27 the second day, 36 the third day, and 18 the last day. When Ike departed Augusta, his cold was gone.

While Ike was still basking in the glow of his successful meeting with the country's biggest foe, he got hit broadside with an attack from a former ally. A book written by British historian Sir Arthur Bryant titled *Triumph in the West* contained the diaries of Lord Alan Brooke, who was Britain's World War II Chief of the Imperial General Staff. The diaries contained some scathing charges about Ike; for instance, "General Eisenhower was 'no commander'...had no strategic vision, was incapable of making a plan or of running operations when started." Another concerned Ike's activities shortly before the Battle of the Bulge.

"General Eisenhower was on the golf links at Rheims–entirely detached from the war."

Shortly after Alan Brooke's diary made news, Hagerty and the White House press operation was making sure that the media knew that the links that Alan Brooke was referring to was actually the clubhouse of the country club at Rheims, the same location where Ike first met gang member Bill Robinson. And that by the time Ike began using it as his headquarters, the course had long since been made unplayable as the result of bombing and artillery fire.

In early December, Ike began an 18-day goodwill trip to 11 countries. The trip was the first time an American president had traveled in a jet-powered Air Force One. The trip included stops in India, Greece, Pakistan, Afghanistan, Turkey, Iran, and Italy. Ike was well received at all the stops as crowds in the millions turned out to see him.

A smaller crowd was waiting to greet him when he returned to the White House. Mamie had arranged for gang members Bill Robinson and Ellis Slater and Alfred Gruenther, a retired Army general who was considered one of the best bridge players in the country, to be waiting for Ike at a bridge table when he stepped out of the elevator and into their private living quarters.

When he exited the elevator, Ike acted as if he had just returned from the corner store instead of a 22,000-mile trip, and joined the group at the table. Unfortunately the bridge would have to wait for another time. Ike's arrival had been several hours behind schedule and it was now past midnight. Despite the late hour, Ike did spend an hour telling the gathering about his trip. Two days later, he and Mamie flew to Augusta for a 10-day stay.

Ike returned to Washington from Augusta on January 5th. Four weeks later, he took a mini golf vacation to LaQuinta, California, and stayed at the new vacation home of George Allen. The trip was to last only three days but Ike decided to extend it to four days once he got there. In late February, he made a goodwill tour to Latin America with stops in Brazil, Uruguay, Argentina, and Chile. Ike got in some golf in Brazil. He made a stopover in Puerto Rico and played three rounds. Two of those rounds took place at the famous Dorado Beach Country Club, where longtime Augusta National golf professional Ed Dudley was now working.

When Ike returned to Washington, his primary focus was on his upcoming trip to the Soviet Union that summer. There had been a story in *The New York Times* in early January that hinted that the construction of the golf course there was coming along. If Ike had wanted to check on the progress himself, he certainly had the means to do so.

As it had on most Americans, Pearl Harbor had had a deep effect on Ike. He believed that it was imperative to know what one's biggest adversary was up to militarily. Just over 60 days after Ike took office, Joseph Stalin died, and the whole Russian hierarchy was in turmoil and the need for solid intelligence increased dramatically. To this end, Ike signed off on the development of the high-altitude spy plane—the U-2—in November 1954. The scientists and engineers given the task of taking the plane from the drawing board to the skies over the Soviet Union were assigned office space in the Executive Office

Building next to the White House. They worked practically around the clock to get the project off the ground. During late afternoon breaks from their labor, they would often look out their office window and see Ike working on his 8-iron shots on the South Lawn.

After the plans were completed at the Executive Office Building, the plane was secretly built by the Lockheed Corporation in California. A Lockheed test pilot was given the task of finding a suitable location for the testing of the plane. He picked a remote spot near Grooms Lake, Nevada. It was located on the edge of the Nevada nuclear test site. This location would later become known as Area 51.

In May 1956, the first U-2 made its maiden flight over Communist-occupied territory and was an immediate success. The Soviets immediately detected that they were being over flown but they did not have a missile capable of shooting down the high-flying intruder.

On Sunday, April 11, 1960, Ike was itching to get down to Augusta for his annual week-after-the-Masters vacation. How soon he would be able to scratch that itch would depend on a former member of the United States Coast Guard he was watching on his television at the White House. The individual whose actions the President of the United States was so keenly interested in was Arnold Palmer.

Palmer was trying to win the Masters for the second time. He had led the first three rounds of the tournament, but as he prepared to play his approach shot to the par-four 18th, he was in a tie with Ken Venturi, who had already finished his round. If Palmer parred the hole, he and Venturi would go at each other in an 18-hole playoff the following day and Ike's Augusta vacation would be delayed for 24 hours. Palmer's 6-iron approach shot produced a loud roar at the 18th green and most likely a single loud cheer at the White House, as it came to rest just six feet from the hole. He then drilled his putt into the cup for a birdie and the win, freeing up the President of the United States to depart for his favorite golf haven.

Ike played a lot of shots during his April stay at Augusta and probably took a few mulligans. For those not familiar with the term, a mulligan is when a golfer is given the opportunity to replay a poor shot without penalty. In early April, Ike made a decision that would have to be the one decision over all other decisions he made during his presidency for which he would have loved to have been granted a mulligan.

The U-2 spy plane was getting its job done, and in the very near future, the U.S. would have satellite capability that could take its place. The Soviets were still believed not to have a missile capable of hitting the U-2. Each mission of the U-2 had to be signed off on by Ike and he was getting more than a little edgy about the operation. He knew the situation with the Russian missile program would not last forever. With a summit meeting with Khrushchev scheduled in Paris in May, and his trip to the Soviet Union to take place later in the summer, Ike was reluctant to authorize more U-2 flights.

Shortly before his mid-April trip to Augusta, the CIA had pressed Ike for one more U-2 run over the Soviet Union. He grudgingly approved the mission, but stipulated that it had to be completed in two weeks. Unfortunately, bad weather over the Soviet Union kept the U-2 on the ground, and the two-week window for the flight expired. On April 25, 1960, four days after Ike returned from Augusta, the CIA requested an extension on the mission, and Ike gave them an additional seven days to conduct the flight.

On Sunday morning, May 1, Ike and George Allen had been driven from Camp David to Gettysburg to play golf, but because of rain, they never got off the first tee. Approximately 10 hours earlier, pilot Gary Powers and his U-2 spy plane had been delayed on the runway at an air base in Turkey for almost an hour. Unfortunately for Ike, Powers did get off, and he was now on the ground in the Soviet Union in the custody of the Russian military. Ike and Allen had returned to Camp David from Gettysburg and had taken advantage of a break in the weather to work on their short irons on the mini-course there. They then did some skeet shooting. It was during the shooting session that Ike received word Powers' U-2 was overdue and most likely down in the Soviet Union.

Ike had always been told that the U-2, despite its high-flying capability, was a very fragile bird, and that if one were ever hit by a missile, the pilot and the equipment on board would never survive. Since Ike and his team did not know for sure what had happened to the plane, they had the National Aeronautical and Space Administration issue a press release stating one of their weather planes was missing on a flight that had taken place near the Russian border. The release also stated that during the last radio contact with the plane, the pilot had reported having trouble with his oxygen supply.

Khrushchev was laughing while Ike and his team were digging themselves into a very big hole. For several days, he kept quiet the fact that they had shot down the U-2 and had Powers in their custody, while Ike kept up his normal work and golf routines. It appeared to Ike that he was going to get out of the situation without any major damage. Then Khrushchev dropped the bomb. He announced to the world that they had shot down the plane and that the pilot was alive and in Soviet custody. Ike had to admit to the U-2's activities over the last five years and that he had attempted to mislead the country and the world with the weather plane story. A few days later, Ann Whitman noted in her diary that shortly after arriving in the office that morning, Ike had told her he was considering resigning. But during the day, his spirits improved greatly, and by late in the afternoon, he appeared to be his old self as he went to the South Lawn for a session with his 8-iron.

Over the next 10 days before their scheduled summit meeting in Paris, Khrushchev was bashing Ike in the press, charging repeatedly that Ike cared more about golf than peace. Ike was still determined to go to the summit, hoping he could somehow reconstruct a dialogue with Khrushchev. When Ike got to Paris, he knew Khrushchev was going to try to make him grovel, and he hoped he would get a chance to speak first, so he could attempt to put his own slant on the situation. But when the meeting started, Khrushchev got the jump on him, quickly rising to his feet, and began railing against Ike and the United States from what appeared to be a mountain of prepared text. He concluded his long tirade by stating that the summit should be postponed for six to eight months—by which time Ike would be not a lame duck, but a political dead duck—and that he was withdrawing his invitation to Ike. He was no longer welcome in the Soviet Union. Despite resuscitation efforts by the French and British, the summit conference quickly died and a disheartened Ike returned home.

Ike filled in the open spot on his schedule due to the cancellation of the Soviet Union trip with a goodwill trip to the Philippines, Japan, Formosa (now Taiwan), and South Korea.

Alaska and Hawaii had been added to the Union earlier in 1959. Ike made stops in those two states on the trip as well, visiting in Alaska on the way out and Hawaii on the return trip. While in Alaska, local officials presented Ike with some items that would today bring a sharp rebuke from animal rights activists: a sealskin bag filled with golf tees made from walrus tusks.

Ike's next stop was in the Philippines, where he had served under General Douglas MacArthur 25 years earlier. Ike received a warm welcome there but the same could not be said for press secretary Jim Hagerty, who was 2,000 miles away in Tokyo. Hagerty and an aide had gone on ahead to Japan to do some work there in advance of Ike's arrival. Japanese Communists had been tipped off to Hagerty's arrival. When his car exited the airport grounds, it was surrounded by a mob of protestors, there to voice their disapproval of a proposed security treaty between Japan and the U.S. They began beating on the vehicle and chanting "!#! #!#! Ike." Hagerty remained calm and actually took pictures of the goings-on with a small Japanese camera until the cavalry arrived, which was a platoon of Marines who were helicoptered to the scene from the American Embassy.

Ike's trip to Japan remained on "go" for a while, but the round of golf Ike had scheduled with the Japanese premier was taken off the schedule for security reasons. But the unrest over Ike's visit continued to mushroom, and two days before Ike was scheduled to arrive, the Japanese premier phoned him and called off the visit.

Ike moved on to Formosa, where he was made an honorary member of the Taipei Golf Club, and then to South Korea, where he received a warm reception. Ike stopped over in Hawaii on the return trip for five days. During his stay he got in five rounds of golf and picked up an honorary degree from the University of Hawaii.

Ike had serious misgivings about Richard Nixon as the Republican nominee for president in 1960. He tried to line up some other candidates to challenge Nixon for the nomination, but he got no takers. After Nixon claimed the nomination, Ike offered his complete support, but Nixon did not take full advantage of the offer; he wanted to put some distance between himself and Ike to show the voters he was his own man.

Just over a month before Election Day and 11 days short of his 70th birthday, Ike became the oldest man ever to occupy the White House. He eclipsed the record held by Andrew Jackson, who was 69 years, 11 months, and 19 days old when he left office in 1837. When he was asked how he was able to cope with the rigors of the presidency, Ike offered this prescription: a round of golf whenever he could get away, no smoking, an occasional scotch highball, and controlling his temper. On that historic day Ike put in a full morning in the Oval Office and spent the afternoon golfing at Burning Tree.

As the campaign heated up, Kennedy and his running mate, Lyndon Johnson, worked "the golf card" against Nixon. Johnson's campaign speeches below the Mason-Dixon Line almost always included this line: "The only thing the Republicans have used the South for over the last eight years was a golf course to tee off from." Kennedy, not wishing to attack Ike directly because of his high popularity, was a little subtler. He would often modify a line from T. S. Eliot's poem *Choruses from the Rock* when he was addressing crowds during campaign stops: "And the wind shall say: Here were decent people: Their only monument the asphalt road and a thousand lost golf balls."

Concerns about how the Democrats were using his golf as a campaign issue against Nixon resulted in Ike turning down a very prestigious golf honor from the home of golf, The Royal and Ancient Club at St. Andrews. Just as the campaign was heating up, the R & A informally contacted Ike through an intermediary asking if he would look with favor on being nominated to serve as their captain.

The captain's position was created in the mid-1860s and the appointment begins in late September and its term is 12 months. At that time only one American had ever served in the post, Francis Ouimet, the man considered to be the father of golf in America. The annual installation of the captain is held with much fanfare in a ceremony where he hits a drive from the first tee at the Old Course to begin his term during the R & A membership's fall meeting. The duties of the post are to essentially serve as ambassador for the game and to be the figurehead of the R & A's worldwide membership.

Ike was honored to have been asked to serve but he sent word back that he would have to decline because he was uncomfortable in accepting the post in the midst of a presidential election for fear it would end up being fodder in the political arena. He did indicate he would be interested in serving once he had left office.

Nixon had started the race as the clear favorite, but Kennedy gained ground steadily. In Ike's two presidential campaigns, he had declined to debate Adlai Stevenson and he advised Nixon not to debate Kennedy. His reasoning was that Nixon, as he himself had been, was the more widely known candidate and that a debate would give his challenger what he needed the most: more exposure. The four nationally televised debates clearly gave Kennedy a huge boost in the race, and he edged out Nixon in one of the closest presidential elections ever.

Ike took Nixon's defeat as a repudiation of his eight years in office, and after the election, he withdrew to Augusta National for a two-week stay. But as the curtain was coming down on Ike's presidency, it was difficult to argue with the results. For the most part, he had given the nation eight years of peace and prosperity, and when he left office, his job approval rating, according to Gallup, was at 60 percent.

11

FINISHING HOLES

I t was cloudy, damp, and the temperature was hovering in the low 40s on February 21, 1961, in Washington when shortly after noon President Kennedy's limo eased out the White House gate onto Pennsylvania Avenue. Several members of the White House press corps had observed his limo's departure. They immediately sought out JFK's Assistant Press Secretary Andrew Hatcher, who was handling the press briefings that afternoon and quizzed him on where the president had gone. Hatcher replied that all he knew was that the president had gone some place with Senator George Smathers of New Jersey.

Hatcher's response piqued the interest of the entire press corps and they kept pressing for an answer as to the president's whereabouts. An hour later, Hatcher returned to the press room. He apologized for not being more forthcoming earlier about JFK's whereabouts but he had not been authorized to say anything. He had now been cleared to report his location and he announced that JFK was at the Chevy Chase Country Club, playing golf with Senator Smathers and Senator Stuart Symington of Missouri.

One of the hush-hush items of Kennedy's presidential bid was the fact he was a golfer and he got in a few holes during the campaign. The members of the press covering his campaign were asked not to cover his golf and photographers were requested not to take pictures. During one of these hush-hush golf outings at Monterey, California, Kennedy came close to making a hole-in-one.

In an interview soon after the election, Walter Hall, Kennedy's pro at the Hyannis Port, Massachusetts club where he learned the game, described JFK as a "hit-and-run golfer" and stated he had been at the club for 16 years and had never seen him play a full round of 18 holes. He would play seven or eight holes and zoom; he was off to other things.

Hall's assessment of JFK's golf was that he could easily shoot in the 70s if he altered his approach to the game. Hall had made Kennedy's clubs. The set was lighter in weight than normal and included a 2-wood JFK preferred to use off the tee. His typical drives with that club traveled from 225 to 250 yards.

Christopher Dunphy was the Cliff Roberts of the famous Seminole Golf Club, which was near the Kennedy family's winter vacation home near Palm Beach, Florida. He played a number of times with JFK there and described him as one of the most relaxed and composed golfers he had ever seen.

Immediately after his election, Kennedy took a page out of Taft's, Harding's, and Ike's play book and went on a golfing binge before his inauguration. He spent a good bit of the month of December in Florida, playing almost every day. Notables who spent some time with the president-elect on the course during this time were his brother, Robert, his vice-president-elect, Lyndon Johnson, and a man who had voted for Richard Nixon in the election: the Reverend Billy Graham.

Over Ike's two terms in office, the criticism by the press over the amount of time he had spent playing golf had built up steadily. *The New York Times* on December 28, 1960, decided that too much had been made of Ike's golf by the critics and the jesters and voiced the hope that President-Elect Kennedy would not be criticized for teeing it up in the following editorial:

...There have been a lot of jokes about Presidential Golf—some good, some bad. In a drab world we hesitate to say there could ever be too many jokes, but it is just possible that jokes about the President playing golf are in oversupply. We make unusual demands, indeed cruel demands that they sit incessantly in sackcloth studying official documents. The critics and jesters would lose their sport if the President took his recreation indoors as in a game of poker, an evening with a whodunit, previewing a movie or watching a western on television. Mr. Kennedy has been playing golf almost daily in Florida. He apparently enjoys the game. He may not play so well as to suggest a misspent youth, but if he plays only on vacation he will certainly play worse rather than better when he finishes his term in office. This is nothing to worry about. But the nation might well worry its conscience over whether it has been having so much uncharitable fun with Presidential golf that it has made a trip around the course a political liability too great for a President to bear. That would be absurd. Mr. Kennedy cannot afford to let other people dictate how he takes his exercise.

For his Easter vacation in 1961, JFK headed back to Palm Beach. Soon after his arrival he teed it up with his father, Joseph Kennedy, and his brothers-in-law, actor Peter Lawford and Stephen Smith. On his tee shot, JFK hit a severe hook that struck a Secret Service agent who was positioned off the fairway's left side. The agent was taken to the hospital to be checked out and returned to his duties later that afternoon. Republicans who had been ravaged by Democrats for Ike's golf were quick to point out this trip to the course by JFK put him one trip to the course ahead of Ike at the same time in his presidency.

Two weeks later JFK was spending the weekend at the northern Virginia farm he was using as a retreat. On Sunday morning, he was playing golf with his sister, Jean, and her husband, Stephen, but his mind was very much on Cuba. He was scheduled to give by noon that day the final go-ahead for the Bay of Pigs invasion. A force of Cuban exiles trained and supplied by the United States was going to land on Cuba's south coast in an attempt to overthrow Castro's government. JFK struggled with the decision as to whether to go through with it. At 2:00 in the afternoon, two hours after the time he said he would give the go or no-go command, he called his Secretary of State, who was his conduit for the operation, and gave him the go-ahead. Shortly after giving the order, he went outside with his two-wood and hit golf ball after golf ball into an adjoining cornfield.

The operation was a disaster, with most of the invasion force captured or killed. As a debacle, it was a 10 on a 10-scale. A week later, Kennedy asked Ike to meet with him at Camp David to go over the ill-fated operation. The two went for a long private walk on the grounds, and went over what had happened. As they were parting ways after their meeting, JFK suggested they should get together for a game of golf in the near future. A few weeks later, however, Kennedy's trips to the course came to an almost complete halt when he seriously aggravated a back problem while participating in a tree-planting ceremony in Ottawa, Canada. And as a result, his outdoor activities were primarily restricted to boating. The back problem kept Kennedy from matching Ike's golf numbers but it did not keep him from outpacing Ike's numbers in vacation days. *U.S. News and World Report* did a study of the two's vacation days in their first nine months in office and found JFK had out-vacationed Ike 78 days to 72. They conducted another study a year later and found at the 21-month mark JFK was still in the lead with a cumulative total of 185 vacation days compared to Ike's 179.

Two big adjustments the Eisenhowers had to make after Ike's presidency involved travel and security. With the presidential plane no longer an option, Mamie's fear of flying often posed some challenges for Ike. One shining example of this problem occurred during a stay at Augusta National when Mamie took a notion to go visit the George Humphreys at their plantation down at Thomasville, Georgia. It was a 200-mile trip south by private plane. But Mamie had another mode of travel in mind. She wanted to go by train.

To make this happen, Ike sought the aid of Charlie Yates, a longtime Augusta National member. Yates was a protégé of Bobby Jones and in the 1930s had been one of the country's top amateurs. His most noted win had come in 1938 when he won the British Amateur at Royal Troon in Scotland. Yates was vice president of the Seaboard Coastline Railroad Company and he made the necessary arrangements for the trip, which turned out to be no small task. First the Eisenhowers departed the train station in Augusta at four in the afternoon and had to go 140 miles north to Florence, South Carolina. Their car was then placed on a side spur until four the next morning when they hooked on to a train bound for Waycross, Georgia, which was 260 miles to the south. Once in Waycross, they hooked on to another train that took them the final 100 miles to Thomasville. They arrived there at two o'clock in the afternoon. It had taken about 12 times longer by rail than it would have taken by air. But Ike had gotten Mamie to where she wanted to be by the means she wanted to get there.

Soon after Ike left office, Congress restored his rank to five-star general, which entitled him to have three military aides: Colonel Bob Schultz; his valet, Sergeant Moaney; and a driver. Unfortunately, at the time he left office, former presidents were not given Secret Service protection. So in regards to his personal security, Ike was on his own. He and Mamie were dividing their time between Palm Springs, California; Augusta, and Gettysburg. It was in Gettysburg that they had the most security problems. With the farm being next to the battlefield, a number of tourists felt obligated to drop by Ike's farm just to say hello. Not all the visitors fell into the tourist class as on two occasions, men who were in the deranged category came a calling.

As the letter below details, this lack of protection was one of the chief reasons Ike eventually backed out of his plans to serve as the Captain of St. Andrews Golf Club:

February 4, 1961

Dear Mr. Grace:

I have just received from The Lord Cohen a letter telling me that the past Captains of the Royal and Ancient Golf Club of St. Andrews desire to nominate me as Captain for the year 1961-62. It would be difficult indeed for me to express the sense of distinction and honor that I feel in the receipt of such an invitation. Unfortunately, I have no recourse but to decline.

A word of explanation would seem due to you. I had assumed during the latter stages of my tenure of the Presidency that my life would become more simple and I would personally be allowed a greater degree of freedom. Actually I have found that with the removal of the traditional protection mechanisms and staffs of the Presidency the demands upon my time, as well as a health problem in my family, further limit my freedom of movement. For these reasons, which I had not foreseen when I talked to the British Embassy in Washington some months ago, I cannot, several months in advance, commit myself to a fixed engagement that under other circumstances I could freely make. Since the obligations of the Captain are such as to commit him to such engagements, I deem it only fair to the past Captains to express my regrets.

I assure you that I shall maintain the private and confidential character of the invitation and shall not reveal any information concerning it. And I assure you again that I am deeply honored by the decision of the past Captains and I send to them an expression of my gratitude and thanks.

Sincerely

Dwight D. Eisenhower

Despite the security concerns, which changed for the better in 1965 when Congress passed legislation that gave Secret Service protection for former presidents, Ike's first years of retirement were very active ones. He was busy writing his memoirs and magazine articles, giving speeches, and playing plenty of golf and bridge. He did not have to look very hard for playing partners, as the gang stayed as active in the post-presidency years as they did while he was in office. But the gang did suffer a devastating blow in March of 1962, when they lost Pete Jones. He was on the way to Palm Springs to meet up with Ike and several gang members for a fishing trip to Mexico but his American Airlines flight crashed moments after taking off from New York City's LaGuardia Airport. Jones and the other 94 people onboard were killed. True to his fetish for carrying large amounts of currency, on his person and in his personal effects was a total of $62,000 in cash. When Cliff Roberts was asked by a reporter if he was surprised Jones would have had been traveling with such a huge amount of money, Roberts stated he was surprised; surprised it wasn't more.

In May 1964, Ike, at age 73, played for the first time in front of a paying gallery. The occasion was a fund-raiser for the Pennsylvania Heart Association. The locale was the famed Merion Golf Club in Ardmore, Pennsylvania, the site of numerous major golf championships. Ike's playing partner was Arnold Palmer. He and Arnie had first met in 1958, and the two soon developed a very strong friendship. Their opponents at Merion were three-time Masters Champion Jimmy Demaret and actor Ray Bolger, who had played the Scarecrow in *The Wizard of Oz*. The two teams squared off in a match play alternating shot format before a crowd of approximately 600 people.

Ike and Arnie took the match, and after it was all over, Arnie addressed the crowd, telling them his partner had carried him all day—and that was no exaggeration. By 73-year-old standards, Ike had given a superb performance. He had looked a little rough on the practice tee, and before heading for the first tee, he had had to gulp down some aspirin for his bursitis.

But once the match was on, the competitive spirit that had been his trademark throughout his life kicked in. He split the fairway with a 220-yard drive on the first hole. Arnie played the next shot to within 10 feet of the pin, and then the crowd roared when Ike drained the putt for an opening birdie and a quick one-up lead. On the eighth hole, Arnie's errant tee shot ended up in the rough and put the team in a bit of a tight spot. But Ike came through in the clutch: he hit a short iron from a hanging lie, over water and over a bunker. The shot came to rest three feet from the pin to set up another birdie, which gave him and Arnie a three-up lead. Demaret and Bolger rallied, and after the 10th hole, they had cut the lead to just one.

On the way to the 11th green, Ike paused to study a plaque that read, "On Sept. 27, 1930 on this hole, Robert Tyre Jones, Jr. completed his grand slam by winning the U.S. Amateur Championship." Reading about the heroics of his great friend must have inspired him. Ike set up successful birdie putts by Arnie with his approach shots at 13 and 15, which once again put them three up. When the two teams halved the 16th hole, the match was officially over as Demaret and Bolger were three holes down with only two holes left to play.

Ike's aide, General Robert Schultz, asked him if he was ready to call it a day. Ike's reply was, "To heck with it; let's finish it." Ike then treated the gallery to two more splendid shots. On the 17th, he snaked in a 45-foot putt for birdie, and on 18, he set up a birdie attempt for Arnie with another fine approach shot.

Ike's play had to have surprised Arnie that day and Ike gave Arnie another big surprise two years later. Arnie's wife, Winnie, asked Mamie and Ike to come to the Palmer home in Latrobe, Pennsylvania, for a weekend as a surprise birthday present for her husband. When Arnie answered an unexpected knock on the door, he was floored. There stood Ike, who said, "Happy Birthday, Pro." Arnie later described that weekend as one of the most special of his life. Mamie and Winnie went shopping, while Arnie and Ike hung out in Arnie's den watching football games and swapping stories.

In the fall of 1965, Ike went to Augusta National for an extended stay. A party in honor of his 75th birthday was held, and some 90 people from all over the country gathered. It was a very enjoyable time, and Ike was in good spirits and good health, but things were about to change quickly.

In his final report on Ike's recovery from his Denver heart attack in February 1956, Dr. Paul Dudley White had predicted the chances of Ike having five to 10 more productive years were very good. At the time, many observers were skeptical. They thought Dr. White was just giving Ike cover to run for a second term. As it turned out, Ike missed the outer limits of the prognosis by just a few months. In the early morning hours of November 9th, in the Eisenhower Cabin at Augusta National, Ike suffered another heart attack. Mamie summoned their Secret Service protection and the club manager, and they got Ike to the hospital at nearby Fort Gordon in short order. Ike bounced back as well as could be expected, but the doctors curtailed his work schedule (public appearances and writing) and limited his golf to par-three courses. Under the new limitations, his health was fairly good for almost the next two-and-a-half years.

In retirement, Ike had become a regular at the 18th green at the Bob Hope Desert Classic in Palm Springs. His presence went off without a hitch until the last tournament he attended in 1968. Tournament officials had decided to honor Ike at the conclusion of the final round by having a combined band from the Navy, Air Force, and Army march down the 18th fairway and then serenade the former Commander-in-Chief with a selection of his favorite songs.

When the tribute was planned, no one factored in what to do if there was a playoff, and that is just what happened. Deane

Beaman and Ike's good friend, Arnold Palmer, finished the event tied for the lead. They went back to the 14th hole to start the playoff as the band came marching down the 18th fairway. Tournament officials became concerned the band would disrupt the playoff, but Arnie made sure his good friend's special moment was not spoiled, as he took the playoff with a birdie on the 16th hole.

A couple of weeks later, on February 6, 1968, at the par-three course at Seven Lakes Country Club in Palm Springs, the golf gods, who had given Ike very close friendships with two of the game's immortals, Jones and Palmer, and a "cabin" at Augusta National, shone upon Ike for one last time when he achieved one of the game's great experiences. He scored his first and only hole-in-one at the 104-yard 13th hole. All of the short-iron practice on the White House Lawn, at Camp David, and in other locales finally paid off when his 9-iron tee shot landed on the front of the green and rolled into the hole. Over the next few days, a picture of Ike displaying his famous grin and holding the ball he made the ace with was featured on most of the sports pages in America. The man who had guided the Allies to victory in Europe and had twice been elected President of the United States said the shot had been the thrill of his life. He told reporters, "Ever since the end of World War II, I have been hacking around courses hoping that 'this might be the day.' For once, that 10,000-to-1 shot paid off for me."

Two weeks after Ike's hole-in-one, Lyndon Johnson came to Palm Springs to seek his counsel on the war in Vietnam. The two played a round of golf at Seven Lakes. Johnson was anything but a serious golfer. He didn't play well or often, but he had a hell of a good time. Those who played in his group didn't need sunscreen; they needed an ointment that would thicken their skin, as Johnson loved to rib the other members of the group with comments of a very personal nature. Johnson played mostly at Burning Tree, and he desired to keep the fact he was golfing out of the press. He was often transported to the course in an unmarked car.

That day in Palm Springs, the press was allowed to cover Ike and LBJ's play only on the first and 18th hole. Ike had beaten LBJ like a drum for 17 holes, but with the cameras rolling and a large gallery at 18, the Texan shined. LBJ reached the last hole in regulation and had a two-putt par. Ike missed the green and then missed a short putt for his par. He was visibly miffed that he had allowed Johnson to steal the show at the last hole.

Six weeks after the match with Johnson, Ike suffered another heart attack. He was hospitalized in Palm Springs for almost 30 days. He was then stable enough to be transported to Walter Reed Hospital in Washington. LBJ sent Air Force One out to Palm Springs to bring Ike back to Washington for the last time.

Ike spent the next 11 months in Walter Reed, suffering one medical setback after another, but he never faltered mentally. Visitors always found him alert, brisk in conversations, and at times even exuberant. He yearned to go home to the Gettysburg farm, but he never pressured his doctors to release him. The medical personnel who attended him said that he was the perfect patient.

The woman whose wrath had been activated way back during Ike's first year as president over the dinner at Burning

Tree, Maine Senator Margaret Chase Smith, was a fellow patient at Walter Reed with Ike for a short period. A well-wisher sent Ike a cake and he sent part of it to Senator Smith's room. In return, she soon sent him a dozen golf balls to symbolize her hope he would recover and return to his favorite pastime.

On October 14, 1968, Ike celebrated his 78th birthday. The Army Band gathered on the grounds outside his hospital room and gave him a concert of his favorite tunes. A frail Ike was wheeled to the window. He acknowledged the tribute with a big smile and by waving a small five-star flag. The scene brought tears to the eyes of many in the nation when it was broadcast on the three major network newscasts that evening.

Over the next five months, Ike's condition gradually worsened, but he continued to receive visitors. The arrival in his room of Arnold Palmer and his wife Winnie brought on one of his famous ear-to-ear grins, and he got some big laughs when Bob Hope dropped by with jokes about golf.

On March 28, 1969, Ike died. His body was placed in an $80 military coffin. He was clad in his Army uniform, complete with the trim "Ike Jacket" he made famous. After his funeral service in Washington, he was taken by funeral train back to Abilene for burial.

Approximately 10 days after Ike was laid to rest in Abilene, another Masters Week began in Augusta, Georgia. One would have to expect Ike's spirit was one of the early arrivals, looking for just the right spot to view his first Masters.

EPILOGUE

In January 1969, a few days after his inauguration, Richard Nixon happened to look down at a portion of the floor in the Oval Office. He noticed that Ike had left his mark on it. It was pockmarked from his golf spikes, where he had walked into and out of the office after his South Lawn practice sessions. Nixon had that section of the floor removed and sent to the Eisenhower Library in Abilene, Kansas.

For all practical purposes, Nixon gave up golf while he was president, but he was well aware of the game's popularity with the public. He always called to congratulate the winner of the U.S. Open, and key figures in the game were frequent guests at White House functions.

The Reverend Billy Graham could confirm Nixon was also very attentive to the importance of golf to his friends. During Nixon's first term in office, Graham was traveling in France when he decided to get in a round of golf. Since he had not brought his clubs on the trip, he rented a set from the pro shop at the course he was playing. Graham proceeded to play one of the best rounds of his life with the rented clubs. At the conclusion of his game, he went immediately to the pro shop and tried to purchase the clubs, but the pro shop manager refused to sell them. The next Christmas, the set of clubs Graham had coveted arrived at his residence. Nixon had heard of the incident and had used the sway of the Oval Office to secure them for Graham.

After Watergate forced Nixon to resign, he had plenty of time on his hands and he began to play golf again, teeing it up several times a week at a course near his San Clemente, California, home. One of his aides was a talented golfer and worked with Nixon on his game, and he ultimately shot the best round of his life, a 78.

As more time passed after his resignation, Nixon gradually began to become more active with other pursuits, particularly writing, and he gave up golf.

On his last day in office, Ike had sent Bobby Jones and his wife, Mary, a note thanking them for all the things they had done for him and Mamie during his time in office. Their friendship remained strong in Ike's post-presidency years. Eleven days before he died, Ike sent a telegram to Jones through an aide letting him know that he had not forgotten his birthday and wishing him many happy returns. Whereas Ike had five good years in retirement before his heart began to fail, Jones's spinal condition grew worse almost every day. Despite being in a wheelchair, he continued to work in his law office, putting in about four hours a day. His activity at the Masters was reduced to sitting on the porch of his 10th fairway cabin and listening to the roars of the crowd or watching the action on television in the cabin's bedroom.

Jones lasted longer than anyone thought he would with his condition. He died on December 18, 1971, at the age of 68. When word of his passing reached St. Andrews, play was suspended on The Old Course.

As for the rest of the gang, George Allen came out with an updated version of his book, *Presidents Who Have Known Me.* Originally published in 1952 about his experiences with Truman and Roosevelt, this updated version contained a lengthy section about his friendship with Ike. Ellis Slater also wrote a book about his relationship with Ike titled, *The Ike I Knew.* Although he probably played golf with Ike the least of any of the gang during the presidential years, Freeman Gosden retired to Palm Springs and played golf with Ike almost daily at Seven Lakes Country Club. After Ike's death, Gosden became one of the driving forces behind the building of Palm Springs' Eisenhower Medical Center.

Soon after Ike left office, Bill Robinson found himself out of a job as Bob Woodruff forced him out the door at Coca-Cola. Robinson was instrumental in expanding Coke sales in supermarkets and internationally, but he didn't always have the full support of Woodruff and other key Coke players. He also rubbed many of the distributors the wrong way. One of their gripes was he played too much golf.

Despite the titles he passed out to Coke executives, Woodruff always kept a firm hand on the operation of Coca-Cola until his death at the age of 95 in March of 1985. While on his deathbed he gave the go-ahead for a change in his soft drink's formula and for it to carry a new name: "New Coke." The move was initiated to fight off Pepsi, which had been gaining market share at a robust rate. The new formula was sweeter, flavored more like Pepsi, and even beat Pepsi in taste tests. But die-hard Coke drinkers were enraged.

New Coke lasted only 79 days before the decision was made (after Woodruff's death) to go back to the original formula. New Coke did earn a spot in history, however, as one of America's greatest marketing failures.

Cliff Roberts continued to run Augusta National with an iron hand until he committed suicide in September 1977. During Ike's recuperative stay at Augusta National in 1949, Ike had taken a walk on the grounds and found a spot he thought would be ideal for a fish pond. He made the suggestion to Roberts and in short order the pond became a reality. It was on the bank of this pond that the then-terminally ill 84-year-old Roberts chose to end his life with a pistol shot to the head.

Roberts, Pete Jones, and Woodruff left major legacies. Roberts was a strong believer in population control. He once reportedly denied membership to Augusta National to a man because he had five children. He left the bulk of his multimillion-dollar estate to Planned Parenthood.

Pete Jones established the W. Alton Jones Foundation in 1944 "to promote the well-being and general good of mankind throughout the world." It is based in Charlottesville, Virginia, has an endowment in excess of $300 million and much of its focus is directed at environmental issues.

Bob Woodruff started The Robert W. Woodruff Foundation in 1937. It has a broad charter to support charitable, scientific, and educational activities. Its grants are generally limited to organizations that are located and operate in the state of Georgia. The foundation has assets of almost 2 billion dollars.

Ike paid tribute to the gang in his memoir *At Ease*, published in 1967: "It is almost impossible for me to describe how valuable their friendship was to me. Any person enjoys his or her friends; a President needs friends, perhaps more intensely at times than anything else."

In November 2009, Ike was inducted into the World Golf Hall of Fame in St. Augustine, Florida. Shortly after the announcement of Ike's selection, Arnold Palmer said this:

One would be hard pressed to find any single person who did more to popularize the game of golf, not only in the United States but throughout the world, than President Eisenhower. His visibility, coupled with his passion for the game, were the inspiration for literally millions of people picking up the game for the first time. Those involved in golf today owe him a great debt of gratitude. Since I was fortunate enough to have enjoyed a warm, personal friendship with the President, I had the opportunity to see firsthand his passion for the game and the impact he had on its broadening appeal worldwide.

ACKNOWLEDGMENTS

This book would not have been possible, if it were not for the superb cooperation from the staff of Eisenhower Library in Abilene, Kansas, especially Herb Pankratz, the archivist who assisted me during my two most enjoyable visits to Abilene. Herb provided me with cart after cart filled with boxes of documents. His knowledge of the library's collection and his suggestions saved me countless hours.

I would also like to thank the Columbia University Oral History Project, the Kansas State Historical Society, and Mary Goodfoot at the Gettysburg Public Library.

Further thanks goes to Elizabeth Ridley at the Writers Midwife and Salem Rana at Burning Frog prods. Elizabeth edited the book. In addition to her superb editing skills, she is a history buff and provided me with some much welcomed insight. Salem handled the book's design, both cover and internals. His talent and professionalism made working with him a true pleasure.

The undertaking of this project was propelled by the assistance and encouragement of some very special people: Ron Labbe, Dr. Cordell Scott, John Ratteree, and my sister, Frances Alewine.

I am also very blessed to have two great sons, Brett and Brandon. Who despite their professional and family responsibilities, could always managed to find the time to give the Old Man a hand when he needed it.

Finally, my greatest appreciation is for my wife Susan whose love and support has buoyed me throughout this undertaking.

BIBLIOGRAPHY

Adams, Sherman. *First Hand Report: The Story of the Eisenhower Administration.* New York: Harper Bros., 1961.

Allen, Frederick. *Secret Formula: How Brilliant Marketing and Relentless Salesmanship Made Coca-Cola the Best-Known Product in the World.* New York: Harper Collins, 1994.

Ambrose, Stephen E. *Eisenhower the President.* New York: Simon and Schuster, 1984.

------ *Eisenhower: Soldier, General of the Army, President Elect*

Anthony Carl Sferrazza. *Florence Harding: The First Lady, the Jazz Age and the Death of Americas Most Scandalous President.* New York: Morrow, 1998.

Bass, Jack and Thompson, Marilyn W. *Ol' Strom: An Unauthorized Biography.* Marietta, GA, Longstreet Press, 1998.

Beschloss, Michael R. *Mayday: Eisenhower, Khrushchev and the U-2 Affair.* New York: Harper & Row, 1986.

Brendon, Piers. *Ike: His Life and Times.* New York: Harper and Row, 1986.

Coletta, Paolo E. *The Presidency of William Howard Taft*, Lawrence, KS: The University of Kansas Press, 1973.

Davis, Kenneth S. *Soldier of Democracy: A Biography of Dwight Eisenhower.* Garden City, New York: Doubleday, 1945.

Donovan, Robert J. *Eisenhower the Inside Story.* New York: Harper & Bros., 1956.

------- *Confidential Secretary: Ann Whitman's 20 years with Eisenhower and Rockefeller.* New York: E. P. Dutton, 1988.

Downs, Randolph Chand. *The Rise of Warren Gamabiel Harding.* Columbus, OH: Ohio State University Press, 1970.

Eisenhower, David. Eisenhower: *At War 1943-1945.* New York: Random House, 1986.

Eisenhower, Dwight D. *At Ease: Stories I Tell to Friends.* Garden City: Doubleday & Co., 1967.

Eisenhower, John S. D. *Strictly Personal.* Garden City, New York: Doubleday & Co., 1974.

Eisenhower, Susan. *Mrs Ike: Memories and Reflections on the Life of Mamie Eisenhower.* New York: Farrar, Straus, Giroux, 1996.

Ellers, Joseph, C. *Strom Thurmond: The Public Man*, Orangeburg, SC, Sandlapper Publishing, Inc., 1993.

Ferrell, Robert. *Ill-Advised.* Columbia, MO: University of Missouri Press, 1992.

Gilbert, Robert E. *The Mortal Presidency.* New York: BasicBooks, 1992.

Graham, Billy. *Just As I Am: The Autobiography of Billy Graham.* New York, HarperCollins, 1997.

Kornitzer, Bela. *The Great American Heritage: The Story of the Five Eisenhower Boys.* New York: Farrar, Straus, and Cudahy, 1955.

Lasby, Clarence. *Eisenhower's Heart Attack.* Lawrence, KS: University of Kansas Press, 1997.

Lyon, Peter. *Eisenhower: Portrait of a Hero.* Boston: Little Brown and Co., 1974.

Morgan, Kay Summersby. *Past Forgetting: My Love Affair with Dwight D. Eisenhower.* New York: Simon and Schuster, 1981.

Neal, Steve. *The Eisenhowers: Reluctant Dynasty*, New York: 1978.

Nixon, Richard. *In the Arena.* New York: Simon and Schuster, 1990.

Owen, David. *The Making of the Masters*, New York: Simon and Schuster, 1999.

O'Reilly. Kenneth. *Nixon's Piano: Presidents and the Politics of Race from Washington to Clinton.* New York, The Free Press, 1995.

Pendergast, Mark. *For God Country and Coca Cola: The Unauthorized History of the Great American Soft Drink and the Company That Makes It.* New York, Charles Scribner's and Son, 1993.

Perret, Geoffrey. *Eisenhower*. New York, Random House, 1999.

Reeves, Richard. *President Kennedy: Profile of Power*, New York, Simon Schuster, 1993.

Rice, Grantland. *The Bobby Jones Story*. Atlanta, Tupper & Love, 1952.

Roberts, Clifford. *The Story of Augusta National Golf Club*. Garden City, New York: Doubleday & Co., 1976.

Russell, Edward and Candance, *Ike The Cook*, (Allentown, PA:1990)

Russell, Francis. *The Shadow of Blooming Grove: Warren G. Harding in His Times*, New York: McGraw-Hill Book Company, 1968.

Sampson, Curt. *The Masters: Golf, Money, and Power in Augusta, Georgia*. New York: Villard Books, 1998.

Slater, Ellis. *The Ike I Knew*. Privately printed. 1980.

Starling, Colonel Edmund W. *Starling of the White House*, New York: Simon and Schuster, 1946.

Van Gelder, Lawrence, *Ike: A Soldiers Crusade*, New York: 1969.

OTHER SOURCES

Newspapers: *The Washington Post, The New York Times*

Magazines: *Sports Illustrated, Golf Journal, U.S. News and World Report, Time Magazine, The Saturday Evening Post, and Colliers' Magazine*

ABOUT THE AUTHOR

David Sowell has written about golf and golf history for over two decades for numerous publications, including the United States Golf Associations Golf Journal. His 2003 book *The Masters: A Hole-by-Hole History of America's Golf Classic*, was praised by *Library Journal* ("an entertaining read that enthusiasts will enjoy") and Book List ("Sowell gives us the Masters in full flower"). In 2017, he authored *Sarazen: The Story of a Golfing Legend and His Epic Moment*. David resides in Taylors, S.C.

Made in the USA
Columbia, SC
07 November 2021